While the basic principles of marketing, "Awareness, Trials, and Usage," are easy enough to understand, how to apply these principles to running a specialty coffee retail business is not. The underlying reason the application of marketing principles is complex is the simple fact that specialty coffee consumers are both discriminating and demanding. The expectations of these consumers are quite high, and the challenge for new specialty coffee retailers is to meet or exceed them. Buying, reading, and studying *Effective & Essential Marketing for the Specialty Coffee Retailer* is a great first step in understanding how to succeed in the highly competitive specialty coffee retail arena. In today's market, it's not enough to find a good location and invest in a great looking store. To be successful, retailers must also invest in their own education to maximize the return on the capital and personal energy they commit to their business enterprise.

— *Ted Lingle, Executive Director, Specialty Coffee Association of America*

Once again, Bruce Milletto and the folks at Bellissimo Coffee InfoGroup have created the answer for one of the ongoing problems for coffee and teahouse operators: how to win the marketing game. Congratulations on another blockbuster business tool.

— *Ward Barbee, Publisher, Fresh Cup Magazine*

As competition in the specialty coffee industry grows more intense, marketing the independent coffeehouse takes on even more significance. In *Effective & Essential Marketing for the Specialty Coffee Retailer*, Bruce Milletto offers important strategies and timely industry information that can help retailers cross the bridge between "Just Making It" and "Really Succeeding." This book is a valuable tool for both beginning retailers and those looking to compete at a higher level.

— *Jeni Banks, Editor in Chief, Specialty Coffee Retailer magazine*

This book provides a well-rounded introduction and step-by-step guide to marketing one's specialty coffee business. Perfect for independent operators or those who are new to the business, this book enables the coffee shop owner to effectively and competitively market his or her business without the marketing budget of a large coffee corporation.

— *Kate LaPoint, Owner, To The Point Business Imaging*

Effective & Essential Marketing for the Specialty Coffee Retailer is an amazing educational opportunity for any aspiring coffee retailer. The value of the information you will receive for the minimal investment of the purchase price is immeasurable. Over the last 15 years the coffee retail industry has benefited from the unique materials Bellissimo has developed. This book is no exception. No one should consider opening a new coffee retail business without adding this book to his or her reference library.

— *David Heilbrunn, President/Show Manager, Lifestyle Events Inc./Coffee Fest Trade Shows*

As the specialty coffee industry creates higher levels of expectation for Americans looking for a new third place, *Effective & Essential Marketing for the Specialty Coffee Retailer* addresses issues that are tremendously important for starting your coffee business on the right foot. And if you don't start right, it's a whole lot harder to start over! Read this book and you will probably succeed.

— *Donald Harrell, Director of New Accounts, Monin Gourmet Flavors*

This book can save you hundreds of hours and thousands of dollars. *Effective & Essential Marketing for the Specialty Coffee Retailer* is a great source of information for individuals who are entering — or already involved in — the specialty coffee retail business.

— *Joe Mancuso, General Manager, Caffé D'arte*

Bruce Milletto has done it again. In addition to his award-winning videos, training manuals and classes, he has created what is sure to become the definitive guide to marketing your specialty coffee retail operation. His new book, *Effective & Essential Marketing for the Specialty Coffee Retailer*, is a step-by-step blueprint for marketing your retail coffee operation. Whether you own a cart, retail outlet or small chain, the ideas, methods, and tools you will need to market you business are all here.

— *David Dallis, President, Dallis Coffee, Inc.; Past President, SCAA*

I highly recommend Bruce Milletto's *Effective & Essential Marketing for the Specialty Coffee Retailer.* It's perfect for anyone embarking on the exciting journey of opening a new coffee retail establishment — and just as useful for those who are already in business and want to improve their operation. Bruce is a confident and expert guide through the world of specialty coffee; he has made it his life's work. Utilizing just one of the many tips Bruce offers can turn a mediocre business into a highly profitable one.

—*Michael Rubin, CEO, Cappuccine*

From selling whole beans to marketing politically conscious products to training employees, *Effective & Essential Marketing for the Specialty Coffee Retailer* is a must-read for anyone just starting out in the business as well as for those already in the business. Bruce presents all the relevant points in an easy-to-read format that provides the independent retailer with all the essential information needed to execute an effective marketing plan that will help take independent specialty coffee retailers to the next level of success.

— *Laura Everage, Managing Editor, The Gourmet Retailer*

Milletto uses his superior expertise to guide readers toward their stores' success with easy-to-follow marketing strategies.

— *Jane Phillips McCabe, Editor & Co-Publisher, Tea & Coffee Trade Journal/ Tea & Coffee World Cup*

Bruce Milletto has a long history of providing coffee retailers with relevant educational programs. This latest work is another important educational tool from Bellissimo that coffee roasters and retailers can use to improve their niche in the marketplace.

— *David Griswold, President, Sustainable Harvest Coffee Importers; Past President, SCAA*

Bruce Milletto once again hits one out of the park! The information in this book is exactly what the new or potential independent coffee shop owner needs to know, ideally before opening day. From marketing to training, Bruce covers in detail the strategies and techniques that every shop owner should consider and employ. *Effective & Essential Marketing for the Specialty Coffee Retailer* will be required reading in my company — and we are wholesalers. This book will help us be a better supplier and partner to our retail customers.

— *Danny O'Neill, President, The Roasterie, Inc.; Past President, SCAA*

Bruce Milletto is a recognized expert in the specialty coffee industry. He has consistently invested his time and incredible energy in helping our industry grow. *Effective & Essential Marketing for the Specialty Coffee Retailer* is another example of Bruce's passion for the coffee industry. In this book, he communicates in straightforward language the steps to achieving success in specialty coffee. The marketing advice Bruce offers is time-tested. In addition, he stresses that each retailer can take advantage of their own unique abilities and create cutting-edge marketing strategies. Bruce's message of "market yourself and your talents" is a pathway to success.

— *Hatton C. V. Smith, President, Royal Cup Coffee*

I have known Bruce Milletto and worked with Bellissimo since 1997. Bellissimo is an industry leader in the fields of training, education and consulting, and over the years the company has developed invaluable products for both new operators and existing café owners. This book on marketing is no exception. Acting on one paragraph from this book should return the purchase price a hundredfold. Use all the great information in the entire book and imagine the results! All retailers make a few mistakes and wish they had done some things differently; *Effective & Essential Marketing for the Specialty Coffee Retailer* provides the information and education you need to improve your chance for success.

— *Tom Palm, President, Design & Layout Services*

To my dear mother Rhea. You have been an inspiring teacher and mentor. Thank you mom. I love you.

Acknowledgements

First, I have to thank Kris Larson, who has been an amazing individual to work with over the years. She is the lifeblood of my company, and without her Bellissimo would never have gained the respect in our industry that it commands today. Second, I thank Matthew, my son. What a blessing it is to have him with me each and every day. His dedication to Bellissimo and coffee grows each week, and I am proud to name him my heir apparent to continue the fight to promote perfection in the world of retail specialty coffee.

I must also thank the countless other mentors and friends in this industry who over the years have made my journey in coffee a heartfelt pleasure: Brandy Brandenburger, Ernesto Illy, Ward Barbee, Mireya Jones, Chuck Jones, Tom Palm, Ed Arvidson, David Dallis, Kenneth Davids, Kevin Knox, Laura Everage, Mauro Cipolla, and Roberto Pregel. Without their passion, friendship and inspiration, this book would never have been written.

Published in the United States by Bellissimo, Inc.
PO Box 5182, Eugene, Oregon 97405
Tel: 800-655-3955
email: ciao@bellissimocoffeeinfo.com

ISBN: 1-893344-15-0

Library of Congress Control Number: 2004110464

Managing Editor: Kris Larson
Editor: Barbara Shaw
Book Design: Matt Milletto
Illustrations: James Cloutier

Bellissimo, Inc. Web site addresses:
www.espresso101.com
www.specialtycoffeeconsulting.com
www.coffeeuniverse.com
www.virtualcoffee.com
www.coffee-drivethru.com
www.planet-tea.com

Effective & Essential

MARKETING

For The
Specialty Coffee
Retailer

Bellissimo
COFFEE INFOGROUP

A BELLISSIMO COFFEE INFOGROUP PUBLICATION

Contents

Preface

The business section of your local bookstore has several shelves devoted to marketing. An Internet search of the word "marketing" delivers 75 million pages for your perusal. Because marketing is at its core the simple act of conveying information, the "information age" has spawned marketing solutions to every problem imaginable and even to problems we have yet to imagine. How will we get people to buy homes on Mars? Marketing.

And yet, whether it be the owner of a small business or a room full of corporate marketing gurus, the question, "How will we market this?" always feels like it is being asked for the first time in history, and even the most experienced marketer answers that question with her fingers crossed. You can read all 75 million Internet pages on marketing and feel like not one of them addresses the marketing issues you are facing today.

Though marketing professionals prefer to emphasize the creative aspects of their job, marketing is, at the end of the day, an economic endeavor and thus susceptible to the influences of voodoo. Like the connection between tax cuts and job creation, the connection between what PMS colors I use in my advertising and increased sales can be, if not suspect, then difficult to track beyond theory. "We know 50 percent of our marketing is effective," says the VP of Marketing, "we just don't know which half is working." I call this The Fog of Marketing.

In *Effective & Essential Marketing for the Specialty Coffee Retailer,* the fog is lifted for coffeehouse operators. Bruce Milletto's coffee-centric look at marketing suffers from neither vague, inapplicable, generalities nor the inane theoretical hairsplitting sometimes found in marketing tomes. Over the years, Bruce has helped countless coffee retailers answer the question, "How will we market this?" and he doesn't waste any time writing about the 50 percent that might not work for you.

It doesn't matter how small your company is or how cynical you might feel about the idea of marketing, you're doing it whether you acknowledge it or not. The question is, are you doing it well? Implement only a handful of Bruce's suggestions and the answer will be yes. Beneath all the shiny-shoe lingo, marketing is about selling stuff. If you're in retail, selling stuff is the reason behind everything you do, from the shirt you decide to wear in the morning, to wiping off the counter tops before you leave the store in the evening. Good marketing is about thinking with greater intention and purpose about all the things you do in between...ALL the things you do in between.

Is pulling a perfect shot of espresso good marketing? You bet. Sustained success in coffee must be built on a devotion to craft and quality. But quality in and of itself will never be enough to grow your business, or maintain the business you have, against new competition.

Consider two baristas working at competing coffeehouses. Both are exceptionally talented and committed to the art and science of not only coffee preparation, but roasting as well. Both belong to the United States Barista Guild. Both obsess over their equipment, coffee, and technique, endlessly trying to squeeze the very best out of all three. But while Barista A rarely looks up from his machine, Barista B makes a point of engaging customers. She occasionally offers regular drip coffee drinkers a free shot of espresso, trying to expand their coffee horizons and deepen their appreciation. She learns the preferences of customers so she can make whole bean purchasing suggestions when new coffees arrive. I would put my money on the coffeehouse where Barista B is pulling shots.

The difference between these two baristas is subtle, interior, and super simple. Barista A is focused on serving a great cup of coffee. Barista B is focused on selling a great cup of coffee to the same customer over and over and over again...and to his friends, family, co-workers, and dentist too. Quality and skill being equal, good marketing wins.

Of course, as an executive at The Specialty Coffee Association of America, I feel obliged to note that the best marketing in the world can't help you if the quality of your coffee is poor. If you're not buying the best coffee you can find, whether you're buying green coffee or roasted coffee, this book won't help you much unless it first convinces you to buy great coffee and then train, train, train your staff. If you purchased this book looking for a few good marketing tips while cutting quality corners, do us all a favor and put the book on the shelf and spend 12 months focusing on improving quality in every aspect of your business except marketing before you pick it up again. I just might walk into your coffeehouse one day and I would hate to have to write on a comment card, as I have on occasion, "Great logo, too bad about the coffee."

On the other hand, if you are quality-obsessed about everything except marketing because you imagine marketing to be "all sizzle and no steak," that's okay. Turn to the title page of this book, cross-out the word "Marketing" and write in its place, "Customer Communication and Education." Better? Good. Now go sell a lot of really great coffee.

July 2004
Mike Ferguson
Chief Communications Officer
Specialty Coffee Association of America

Introduction

I started to write this book in a hotel in Bend, Oregon on a snowy day in the winter of 2002. The need for such a volume had been apparent to me for many years, but I also knew the act of writing it would take more time than I felt I had available. That day I dissected marketing and how it relates to the specialty coffee industry and created the rough outline that spawned this book.

Some coffee retailers are fortunate enough to have the ability to "think marketing" every waking moment, some are not. The lucky ones understand innately that almost everything you do in a retail operation contains at least one major component of marketing. As you will see in these 20 chapters, facets of retail you may have thought weren't even related to promoting your business are actually vital components of your overall marketing program.

When I travel and visit retail shops across America and around the world, I frequently see small and inexpensive ways in which these operations could be made better. Some of them need major damage control. But we will never live in a perfect world. There will always be those among us who simply don't care or don't understand the importance of striving for perfection. These individuals only want to make money and will never realize their businesses won't be truly successful without passion and dedication.

Each retailer has a slightly different breed of dragon to slay to be successful. I sincerely hope that after you finish this book, you will feel inspired and motivated to know and truly understand that you can successfully market your business. But to achieve this goal, you must adopt the title of one of the chapters in this book as your mantra: "Everything Must be Perfect."

CHAPTER 1

WHY MARKETING WORKS

Believe it or not, there are actually business consultants in the specialty coffee arena who will tell you that marketing is a waste of time. I say, get real! If you don't market and advertise wisely, your chance of success in coffee, tea or any other business is slim to none. Circus master P. T. Barnum summed it up ages ago. "Without promotion something terrible happens — nothing." No matter who your customers are, what you sell, where you locate, what your economic objectives or what values you bring to doing business, without marketing all your hopes fall flat.

It's a truism that word of mouth is your best advertising. What people tell their friends and co-workers about their experience will make or break you. If they rave about your business, their approval is worth huge profits for you. If they shake their heads, you're doomed. That you strive for perfection is non-negotiable. If you yearn to win loyalty and love from great customers, you have to make them say "Wow." But to get them interested, you have to make the first move.

In the coffee business, most cookie-cutter concepts don't work.

The first step in making sure your marketing efforts work is to get personally excited about promotion. Believe me, nearly anyone who can run a business can and must do this. In the coffee business, most cookie-cutter concepts don't work, which is great. That opens up the opportunity for creativity and for giving your operation a unique identity. What kind of fool would design the same interior and menu for a coffee operation in Hawaii as for a shop in Maine?

Bellissimo worked with a client in a shopping plaza in a posh resort in Arizona. Because of the hot climate, we helped him develop a very "site-specific" menu that included more cold coffee drinks than usual. In addition, we created a menu of signature drinks and named them after the local mountains and desert — the "Camelback Cooler" and the "Mojave Iced Mocha."

The decor was designed for those steeped in the Mercedes lifestyle and blended an Arizona theme with upscale creature comforts. Once open, I suggested this client ask local spas and hotels to distribute flyers and maps designed to lure customers to "The Best Cappuccino in the Entire Southwest." How could a chain or franchise compete, if stuck with management, purchasing and training decisions made at the corporate office on the opposite coast?

There's no denying that the major chains have name recognition and buying power, a couple of advantages you lack. But out of necessity, they usually run their stores the same way in Manhattan as they do in Iowa. Use this to your advantage. If you are in Iowa and bucking huge advertising dollars by the Big Chain, use fun phrases in your marketing like "The Delightful Des Moines Difference," "Iowa's Prairie Home Latte" or "Corn Fed Cappuccino."

Bottom line, take advantage of the fact you are an independent. You have the power and flexibility to make your own decisions and tailor promotions to your community. Smaller chains can let location directly influence how they market their concept in a given area, especially if their franchise or licensing agreements have flexibility that allows an owner to do specific marketing approved for their location. This is smart.

Other than a couple of huge chains, most coffee chains are regional. Go to cities like Chicago, Phoenix or Cincinnati and ask people on the street to name four big coffee chains. It's likely they will only be able to come up with one. Ask the same people to name four major hamburger chains, and most would be able to rattle off McDonald's, Burger King, Wendy's and Jack in the Box. Only one coffee chain benefits from national name recognition and its corresponding marketing punch. That helps you make a big local name for yourself.

If you only see dollar signs, you'll regret going into this business. What's the point of creating a business that turns into a monster or a bore, so you can't live a fulfilling life? Your own goals, and sense of who you are and want to become, must be clear. But let's assume you've already done your inner homework, opened your business and find yourself underwhelmed with customer enthusiasm. Maybe you should advertise and market.

> Bottom line, take advantage of the fact you are an independent.

Today, everywhere we look, we are exposed to advertising. From our cars, we catch sight of highway billboards and city buses transformed into large mobile ads. Subways are littered with signs, planting seeds for us to support sports teams or buy a certain brand of vodka. Log onto the Web and you'll see banner and pop-up ads on almost every page. Everywhere we turn, marketers are pitching us.

As annoying as this bombardment may be, the reason businesses do it at no small cost, is simple. It works! Dozens of companies spend more than $300 million to put up LED and computer-programmed signage in Times Square in New York City to continually remind people to watch the latest sitcom, invest in the NASDAQ or buy Calvin Klein underwear. You can bet their accountants tell them this is a solid investment.

Smart marketing is a sophisticated combination of being in the right place at the right time with the right message about the right products.

Have you sworn you would never eat fast food again only to find yourself tempted after seeing an ad touting the latest and greatest burrito? Really, how many ways can a fast-food Mexican chain present the same product – a tortilla with rice, beans, spicy meat, and guacamole? They do it by marketing. For starters, they come up with a snappy name like "The Cha Cha Cha." Then they hire food stylists and photographers to make this 99-cent fare look like something you can't live without – especially at a quarter of the price you would pay for it at a sit-down restaurant. If you've found yourself passing a fast-food chain where you know the food is a long way from gourmet, and actually stopping to purchase their latest item, like millions of others you were seduced by smart marketing.

Smart marketing is a sophisticated combination of being in the right place at the right time with the right message about the right product. We all know some promotions work well while others don't. It's the job of marketers to balance the variables and convince people to buy. When tens of millions of dollars are involved in national campaigns, it's no job for amateurs. And yet anyone who can read, think, accept feedback and carry through can use smart marketing to increase business share. The secret is to plan, invest wisely, measure the result and continue to make changes until you finally get it right.

On the other hand, marketing may not be your strong suit. If you honestly dread it, have little or no experience and don't get any pleasure from the process, hire a pro. Especially as you get started, beware of the false economy of refusing to invest in expertise. Marketing, advertising and public relations people are highly creative. They have cultivated taste and have spent their entire careers learning all sorts of clever ways to increase your profits. And if you learn enough from them and stay tuned to every resource to educate yourself, you can do part or all of the marketing yourself, later.

Whether you take it on yourself or hire it out, the big marketing challenge for the owner of a single coffee operation is competing with the corporate chains in your area, with advertising budgets hundreds of times what you can afford. When you've read this book, you will have plenty of ideas. But whatever marketing choices you make, you'll have to set aside time every day or week to address this absolute essential of success. And you'll need a budget, preferably in a special account that you can control and use to access your results.

Do your research and find out what it costs to use the various local media — radio, TV, newspapers, weekly papers, direct mail, billboards, signs on buses and trucks, ads in local catalogs and entertainment and sports programs, etc. Do more research and notice all the ways you can get free publicity. Put on an event and invite local TV news crews. Promote coffee-tasting events. Put on programs to educate people about sustainable coffee farming in poor countries. Show up with your coffee at colleges, hospitals, charity events, library book sales, dances, sports events, parades and festivals. Make an effort to donate to your community. Write for local papers using your expertise on such topics as how to choose great beans or the perfect home espresso machine.

> Don't wait until your business is sagging to do your marketing. A concentrated and sustained effort early in the game will give your business the necessary start-up exposure.

Don't wait until your business is sagging to do your marketing. A concentrated and sustained effort early in the game will give your business the necessary start-up exposure. Before you go any further, you'll want a good name, a great logo and a concise business image. See Chapter 12 for more on that. Then comes a detailed plan, a calendar of what to do when, and a promise to yourself to stick to it. A good plan sets goals, targets specific demographics, takes into account the competition, has a clear objective, and selects appropriate media. Whatever you do, be as professional as possible. Your audience will be comparing your efforts to the hundreds of glitzy million-dollar ad campaigns they see each month.

Good marketing is both art and science. It will include creative brainstorming, plus planning months in advance to purchase advertising so you can meet deadlines and keep customers consistently thinking about you. Your specific marketing choices will be determined by who you are and what you offer. Let these guide you as to where to put your efforts and money.

Marketing goals could include getting more customers, keeping the ones you have, getting them in more often and getting people to spend more.

As for the science, research data shows that the average person is exposed to a newly advertised product or business at least seven times before they can recall details and about nine times before they spend money on a new idea. That means you can't expect a brief effort to yield grand results. But you don't have to do it all, or let it overwhelm you. Even so, without a road map, you're lost.

In your planning, be realistic. When we dream of opening a business, we imagine everything functioning perfectly. But reality includes times when numerous aspects may go wrong. Reality will include some of each, so when you look ahead follow your gut and use your best guess as to what is likely to happen in any given scenario.

Marketing goals could include getting more customers, keeping the ones you have, getting them in more often and getting people to spend more — or all of these. This business is dependent on volume — more people, more often, making more purchases. If you sell a muffin to every second customer, you can increase your gross by several thousand a month. Your marketing goals could be quite specific — bringing in more business, meeting customers or creating a promotion to sell 20 percent more beans. You could determine you want to train employees in tactics that will sell 30 percent more pastries between eight and eleven in the morning, or to hand out a coupon to increase sales of gift items by 80 percent during the holiday season, compared to July.

A word to the wise...check with friends, staff and customers for a gut reaction before initiating any marketing program. Refusing honest feedback could be fatal. Your brilliant idea may strike your hip young barista as "dumb." Tweak your ideas until nearly all agree your plan is smart, workable and achievable.

OK, you have this great plan, but how will you know if you succeed? A good accounting system is essential to good marketing. Before you start any marketing effort, use your numbers to establish a base line. How was I doing before this marketing strategy? Then set objectives for your marketing plan. All of your efforts can then be designed to meet your specific objectives. And how do you know if you're meeting your objectives if you can't measure results? A successful marketer keeps accurate records and knows what's working and what's not. If it's not working, analyze why and change your plan of attack.

Many small business owners feel intimidated by competitors. You may be surprised to know that competition is a very good sign. It means there's a market for what you have to offer. The good news is you can compete and, as a wise marketer, you can actually beat your competitors at their own game. When you know your community, offer a unique and distinct product and tailor your promotions to your particular business philosophy, you can attract loyal and happy customers.

Many small business owners feel intimidated by competitors. You may be suprised to know that competition is a very good sign.

By no means would we suggest that you scoff at the competition. You can pick up a lot from the big guys and from the clever gal across town with a thriving little boutique. Analyze what they do better than you, and how you can outsmart them. Look at their customers and their equipment. Study their image and décor. Notice the appearance of their employees and how they behave. If you see a weakness, take note and made sure you're not guilty of a similar faux pas. If you see a brilliant idea, learn and earn from it.

Whatever your deep personal reasons for choosing to open a coffee business, if you plan to survive long term, the ultimate goal has to be healthy sales and profits. Marketing is a proven means to this end. Of course, your business will reflect your own personality. But your dreams will shrivel unless you attract new people to add to a loyal customer base. If you succeed, people will look forward to visiting your business because it appeals to all their senses, inviting them to relax and indulge themselves, tantalizing them with exciting information and possibilities. Provide a clean and friendly place where everything is comfortable and easy — an experience they truly value.

So, how do you create value? Price is secondary. Avoid the bargain basement trap. You are selling desire, not need. You are a retail business, selling a great experience with personal service. Anyone can buy great beans and fine brewing equipment, and make superb coffee at home. So, you are selling far more than good coffee. You are selling a social setting, a pleasant place to meet, human interaction, luxury and comfort. Your coffee business fits the definition, from sociology, of The Third Place. It's not home and not work but a place for connecting with friends and new people. For more reading on that subject, try sociologist Ray Oldenburg's book *The Great Good Place: Cafés, Bookstores, Bars, Coffeeshops, Hair Salons and Other Hangouts at the Heart of Community.*

Just as people gather around the fire to talk in tribal societies, people in the modern world need a gathering place. When a little town loses its café, the whole community is left grieving and without a heart. The gathering place will never go out of style. Today's fast-paced society demands even more places to congregate, meet and visit.

Along with providing a meeting place, your coffee business adds a touch of hedonistic delight. Obviously, nobody "needs" a fancy espresso drink enjoyed in a soft purple chair within earshot of cheerfully chatting strangers. And no one needs a day at the spa or a luxury hotel room overlooking the water. But we do enjoy the extravagance. Self-indulgence makes us feel good. Fine service, quality products, delightful presentation, a variety of options, a sense of status — are all more important than price in how people value what you have created in your coffee business. Charge fair prices, but cover all your costs. And I recommend you know to the penny what your true costs are.

You worked hard during the pre-opening process. You secured a prime location, purchased the best equipment and opened for business full of optimism. But once the doors open, you are only halfway up the hill. You can't coast. Climbing a hill, if you coast you'll soon go backwards. If you pedal twice as hard as you did during your pre-opening fervor, you will succeed in your new business reality — keeping your doors open and your profits flowing.

CHAPTER 2

STAYING ON THE CUTTING EDGE

To stay ahead of your competition, you'll need to change your business to meet the continually shifting demands of the market. After your doors are open, the push for success requires you to persist in your research and adapt what you learn to your operation if you hope to stay on the cutting edge of the specialty coffee industry.

At a meeting of a retail association, the well-respected speaker who had worked in retail his entire life offered the following: "The only thing constant in retail is change. If you refuse to change, your business will die." He shocked me when he used my retail store as an example. He told a large gathering of merchants, "If you want to understand what I mean by this statement, study Bruce Milletto's operation. I have, and he is one of the few who truly understand change. Milletto modifies his displays and merchandising almost on a weekly basis."

Grandiose schemes are not the only way to win. Small and clever can do wonders.

I had never really given merchandising much thought. Keeping my store looking fresh came naturally to me. Unfortunately, it does not come this easily to every retailer. You may develop a great image and marketing strategy today, but it may not be right tomorrow. If change does not come naturally to you, you can learn to keep your store up-to-date and stay on the cutting edge of this quickly changing industry.

Get innovative and aggressive. Check out your competition. Visit the malls and other retail operations. Surf the net. Be poised to catch the next wave. Visit the nearest big city and look for ideas you can add to your operation. Make your business distinct and original. Hand out business cards and brochures wherever you go. Let the media know you love to be interviewed. To thrive at the marketing game, make it part of your life and breath. And keep at it. About the time you're tired of it, the public is just starting to notice.

Grandiose schemes are not the only way to win. Small and clever can work wonders. The owner of a coffee shop in Indiana was one of Bellissimo's early clients. This retailer ran a local newspaper ad with a photo of his nine-year-old granddaughter holding a cup of coffee. The ad read "Brianna Poulson, Age 39. Drinking coffee keeps me young." He added his logo, address and hours. Another ad used a photo of his yellow lab. He runs these ads weekly in the local paper at a cost of about $70. The ads make people smile and have been hugely successful.

Much information to help you stay on top of trends and products is free if you make the effort. Take advantage of the following ideas to stay on top of the game.

Trade Shows

As with most industries, the specialty beverage trade boasts no shortage of conferences and trade shows. But given the diversity and high number of events, deciding which ones to commit to as an exhibitor or attendee can be a daunting task for the average retailer. Most of us can't afford the time and money to attend many of the trade shows in any given year, so it's important to choose those best suited to your operation.

The SCAA Conference & Exhibition

The largest of these shows is the Specialty Coffee Association of America Conference & Exhibition. It features the latest and greatest industry products and trends as well as a diverse cross-section of attendees.

In addition, this show exposes retailers to the green side of the industry, with exhibitors from such coffee-producing countries as Brazil, Mexico, Guatemala, Indonesia and Africa. It's a great opportunity to taste many of the world's specialty coffees and attend seminars given by some of the top presenters in the world. Added excitement comes from both the National Barista Championship and the World Barista Championship, which are held in conjunction with the event. The many after-show parties provide wonderful networking opportunities.

NASCORE

The Portland-based NASCORE Specialty Coffee and Tea Trade Show often holds its annual event in its hometown — one of the hotbeds of specialty coffee. In past years, the show has ventured to San Francisco, St. Paul and New York City. The coffee retailer is the primary focus of this show, with limited attention given to the green side of the business. The show includes hundreds of exhibitors and coffee and tea tastings hosted by industry experts, plus an extensive agenda of seminars on marketing and products. If you're interested in expanding your business to include tea, you'll appreciate the special emphasis of the presentations here. This show is a favorite of mine because of the many evening events open to both attendees and exhibitors.

Coffee Fest

Coffee Fest began over ten years ago as an annual event in the mega center of specialty coffee – Seattle. The show was popular because retailers loved to visit the birthplace of American specialty coffee to see how many new operations had opened in the past year. The first shows in Seattle were so successful that Coffee Fest expanded its operations and today does three shows a year, one each in Seattle, Las Vegas and a city on the Eastern seaboard. Any Coffee Fest offers a show full of impressive exhibits and free seminars. Like the shows mentioned above, Coffee Fest has a night dedicated to a come-one-come-all party that will allow you to network with other owners and to meet many of the vendors in a casual off-the-floor setting.

Other Shows

At the end of the chapter I have listed other shows that could be important to you depending on the size of your business, the amount of food you serve or the size of your retail space. For example, the Fancy Food Show showcases the newest add-on food items and the National Restaurant Association Show features the latest in equipment.

If you can afford to attend, the International shows are fun, though less educational. However, they will teach you about the coffee industry outside the United States and allow you to take a vacation at the same time.

Why Go?

Without testing firsthand, it's impossible to tell how noisy a machine is, how hot the base of a blender gets or how crumbly the biscotti are. Where else could you easily taste five brands of syrups or multiple powder mixes? In this hands-on industry, trade shows are the perfect places to get the feel and taste of numerous products. Plan to attend a few shows if you can in the coming year to keep your operation on top of the newest trends and offerings, and to brush up on your skills and knowledge in workshops and seminars. Above all, enjoy yourself. As exhausting as trade shows can be, the suppliers and friends you'll meet make it valuable time spent and should invigorate you and your business.

The other business owners you'll meet at trade shows, people doing what you are doing, are a rich resource. As long as the two of you are not in direct competition, in the same neighborhood, sharing discoveries is good for business. Talk about your problems, and your brilliant marketing ideas. Ask what's worked for them. Find out what they know about a machine or product you are considering. Share what you've learned and encourage those who are struggling. Even in your own community, joining business organizations and getting to know others in different industries is a great way to learn and grow, and to develop friendships with dynamic self-starters like you.

Plan to attend a few shows if you can in the coming year to keep your operation on top of the newest trends and offerings.

Trade Publications

I cannot overstate the importance of subscribing to each and every coffee-industry trade publication. A number of the most important ones are listed at the end of this chapter. Why would anyone who owns a coffee operation NOT want to stay informed about the latest information the coffee world has to offer?

On a recent business trip, I stopped at a coffee drive-thru in a small town. As the server poured my granita, I asked her if she was the owner, and she said she was. I asked her what coffee magazines she read and she told me she didn't read any of them. I asked her why, and she said she was busy and didn't have the time. "I used to subscribe to a couple," she said, "but the subscriptions ran out and I have not bothered to re-subscribe."

I find it unthinkable that some retailers are unwilling to invest in a magazine subscription in their area of business. Though I find it unbelievable, this attitude is not rare. I have heard similar stories from many retailers. These are often the same retailers that visit Bellissimo's trade show booth or call our office wondering why their sales are stagnant. They can learn how to grow and change, or watch their business die.

Fresh Cup Magazine and *Specialty Coffee Retailer* are the two U.S. magazines dedicated to the coffee retailer. *Tea and Coffee Trade Journal* is also an excellent resource. *Coffee and Beverage Magazine* is devoted primarily to the Canadian market. As a retailer, you should read as many of these periodicals as you can from cover to cover. From the comfort of your bedroom or an easy chair, you can learn about the world of retail specialty coffee and tea for a few dollars a month. Don't pass up this opportunity.

Education Should Be Ongoing

Many great books, videos and DVDs are available to teach you the nuances of specialty coffee.

Never stop educating your staff and yourself. But how do find the information you need? Search out books like this one that speak directly to you as a retailer. Also look for books that offer you general information about coffee.

Many great books, videos and DVDs are available to teach you the nuances of specialty coffee. Bellissimo has produced numerous training products that will help you serve the best product and provide the best customer service possible. Harder to find are books like this one that provide you with up-to-date information that will help you take your business to the next level.

A recent Bellissimo publication does just that. *Achieving Success in Specialty Coffee* contains 23 chapters, each written by a coffee expert, with cutting-edge information based on hundreds of accumulated years of experience. Avail yourself of this wisdom. You want to make as few mistakes in your business life as possible. Learning from others is the best way to avoid pitfalls.

Get Out of Your Store and Open Your Eyes

Wherever you go, look at what other operations are doing and incorporate their best ideas into your own operation. Check out menus, pricing, retail displays and clever layout and merchandising ideas.

I always cringe when I talk to prospective consulting clients who say, "My husband and I want to open a coffee bar exactly like the large chain store in town." I always ask them if they want to copy this store because of the company's success. This is usually the case. I then tell them they should take the chain's best ideas, add their own creativity and build something unique that they can be proud of, an operation that is an extension of their ideas. As a retailer, you would be crazy not to visit the local chain operation on a regular basis to find out what they know that you may not. We will get into this in more detail in Chapter 16, *Marketing Against the Chains*.

Change

Be aware that the coffee market is constantly changing and that you'll need to change with it. Some consultants will tell you marketing is a waste of time and that you should be able to make a profit by selling only coffee. For most operations, following this advice is a recipe for disaster and low check receipts.

When I first got involved in the coffee industry, I gave little thought to marketing or changes in the industry over time. But I quickly learned that just as the stock market changes from month to month and year to year, so must the marketing of a coffee business.

Once, a coffee cart occupied almost every corner in downtown Seattle. Now there are next to none. The market changed, permanently. Today consumers expect more than coffee and a plastic-wrapped muffin or biscotti. They want to choose from a broad menu, and in many instances, they want to sit down and enjoy their selections in a comfortable environment.

Today, drive-thrus are the fast and easy way for consumers to get a quick hit of caffeine. Though they are commonplace today, it was only a few years ago that I approached my local health department with the idea of developing the first drive-thru location in Eugene, Oregon. The official looked at me like I was crazy. This perception has changed over time, and today, the same administrator would probably ask me, "Do you really think there is another corner available for a drive-thru in Eugene?"

> Be aware that the coffee market is constantly changing and that you'll need to change with it.

The coffee business will continue to change and it's important that you and your business are able to change with it. Keep up on current trends, and stay one jump ahead of them — and your competition. REMEMBER "The only thing constant in retail is change... If you refuse to change, your business will die."

Trade Shows

Coffee Fest
800.232.0083
www.coffeefest.com

SCAA Annual Conference & Exhibition
562.624.4100
www.scaa.org

NASCORE
503.236.2587
www.nascore.net

Canadian Coffee & Tea Expo
416.784.5210
www.coffee-expo.com

Fancy Food Show
212.482,6440, ext. 250
www.fancyfoodshows.com

National Restaurant Association
312.853.2525
www.restaurant.org/show

Periodicals

Fresh Cup Magazine
503.236.2587
www.freshcup.com

Specialty Coffee Retailer
773.881.9273
www.specialty-retailer.com

Tea and Coffee Trade Journal
212.391.2060
www.teaandcoffee.net

Coffee & Beverage Magazine (Canada)
416.596.1480
www.coffeeandbeverage.com

The Gourmet Retailer Magazine
847.763.9050
www.gourmetretailer.com

Fancy Food Magazine
888.545.3676 ext 10.
www.fancyfoodmagazine.com

Forum Café (Spain)
www.forum-cafe.com

Coffee & Cocoa International
www.dmgworldmedia.com

Tea & Coffee Asia
www.teacoffeeasia.com

Beverage Retailer
662.236.5510
www.beverage-retailer.com

CoffeeWorld
www.westendpublishing.com

Virtual Coffee
www.virtualcoffee.com

CHAPTER 3

WHO IS YOUR CUSTOMER?

Before you can plot a winning strategy, you have to know who you are talking to. The first step in formulating a successful advertising or marketing campaign is to identify and get to know your target market. You can never know too much about your customers, both the people you count on to spend money and the ones you hope to recruit.

When you are choosing a location, demographic information will provide the first clues if you are not familiar with the people and culture of an area. You might be surprised, for instance, to learn that 40 percent of the people living in the area are under 40, have been there less than two years, work 60 hours a week and earn over $80,000 a year. Or that a large percentage of your customers are retired and like to golf. Near a college, many could be students under 25 into extreme sports. In a small town, half might be people from a rural background who feel uncomfortable ordering drinks with foreign names.

As in any business, before you invest, do your research.

The Bellissimo office sometimes gets calls from individuals in Washington or Oregon who have just returned from a trip, shocked to find little or no specialty coffee in the area. They are considering uprooting their lives and moving to the less coffee-saturated location they visited, to open a specialty coffee business.

Suppose they did move to a latte-free zone? What do they know about the local people? There's a good chance that outsiders will make inaccurate assumptions about the habits, likes and dislikes of the population of an unfamiliar community. As new arrivals, they will have a lot more marketing work to do than a local person who retired from the fire department and now wants to open a coffee business.

Who is Your Customer

As in any business, before you invest, do your research. The term "due diligence" refers to the respectful and serious diligence due any project where significant amounts of money are involved. Anything less than due diligence is guesswork, and gambling with possible bankruptcy. Always do plenty of research.

Let's assume you buy an existing operation. You take a big chance if you assume, without proper investigation, that the area has demographics that will find this concept appealing. That's why most savvy business people don't purchase an existing operation but look for an ideal location, one that suits the ideas, menu, ambiance and character of the business they envision. Often a business that is for sale is being sold for a reason, such as poor location or steadily eroding numbers. It's wise to remember that, in buying a coffeehouse, you may need to overcome years of poor management by the former owners.

At Bellissimo, we talk to people from all sorts of backgrounds who want to open a coffee operation. Some plan to open their business in the inner city. Others tell us they will be opening their store in an upscale strip mall adjacent to a new development with million-dollar homes. I can guarantee that you will approach your marketing quite differently, depending on where you decide to locate your business.

Whatever location you choose, you will have to become familiar with the habits, likes and dislikes of your customers. First, find out the median household income of the area. These statistics are usually available from a local government agency or you often can find them on the Internet. Next, find out how many cars visit the shopping center you have chosen, or drive by your location on the major thoroughfare.

Ask yourself questions. "Why do people visit this particular shopping center? Does it contain stores that will attract the same customers I am targeting?" A good location to consider might be near a busy grocery store or movie complex. If you are in a center that also houses a health-food store or gym, consider marketing that captures the mindset of the health-conscious consumer.

Find Out More About Your Own Customers

The many ways to acquire information all involve research. Well before you open, gather information to make your marketing easier. Ask questions and really listen to the words and body language of the answers. You want to know who is buying and why. If you understand people's motivations, it's far easier to appeal to them with your marketing and to keep them, and others like them, happy. Train your employees to ask leading questions and report to you what customers want.

Your suppliers keep up with the industry and have a vested interest in seeing you grow, so tap into their expertise too. You can't win all the people all the time, but you can win with a certain demographic when you create a unique niche for yourself using decor and special menu items that satisfy your chosen group of customers.

In-house surveys and conversations with customers will provide additional ideas. Some large chains have disclosed that their pre-sold drink cards are one of the primary reasons behind the growth of their business. They sometimes use questionnaires with these cards to obtain other useful information. You could offer a free beverage, or entry in a drawing for a free pound of beans, to those willing to fill out a form.

If you decide to use such a method to gather customer data, choose carefully what you really need too know. Six or eight questions to answer in writing are enough. Include a checkbox where customers can elect to receive information on new products or specials. If you obtain your customers' e-mail and physical addresses, you can send them promotional materials or a newsletter informing them about a new product or special of the month.

Useful things to know about your customers include their age and whether they have children, if they own or rent, if they live nearby or are tourists, their educational level, what kind of work they do and what clubs they belong to. These are clues to socio-economic status and predictors of what standards of excellence or amenities they may demand, what they like and can afford.

You may want to know more. In conversations, you can ask about the customer's favorite drink, additional food and drink they'd like to see offered, favorite place for lunch and why. Ask what kind of environment they like for a break, what musicians and artists they enjoy, their leisure pursuits, and consumption habits — how many cups of coffee per day or how many times a week they patronize a coffeehouse or drive-thru.

Another way to gather information is to hold a weekly drawing for a French press or beans. Ask interested people to drop their business cards or a form into a giant coffee cup or other container on the counter. I will talk about these and dozens of other ideas in Chapters 17 and 18 on guerrilla marketing. The point I want to stress here is that you must know who your customers are. The better you know them, the more effective your marketing can be. The goal is to find a need and fill it, a centuries-old formula for success.

Modern point-of-sale systems will give you a wealth of information about your operation and sales. Study this data on a daily or weekly basis and adjust your operation and marketing from the knowledge you gain from your point-of-sale system.

One additional method for finding out more about your customers is the focus group, made up of 7 to 12 people. Major advertisers and product development people often use focus groups to get information about customer responses. A professional should lead the focus group, to direct the discussion and encourage everyone to be honest. These meetings are often videotaped or sound recorded for review later. The participants are generally paid for their time, usually for no more than two hours.

The leader poses questions for discussion such as, how people view what the business is currently doing, problems they see in the operation and proposed new products. If you use this method, your job is to sit down with the leader and the recording and learn all you can from the feedback offered.

...you must know who your customers are. The better you know them, the more effective your marketing can be.

What are Your Customers' Needs?
What you choose to serve should be directly influenced by your customers' desires and needs. Before you open, you might walk around the area and introduce yourself as the owner of a new business. Boldly ask people what items they would like to see on your coffeehouse menu. You may be surprised by what they tell you. For example, you may have planned to serve little or no food, but you hear from prospective customers that there are no unique lunch spots in the area and they hate to eat fast food. Take this new information as an opportunity to meet the needs of the customers in your particular area. Keep it simple but develop a menu based on your customers' desires.

If you are already open, talk to your customers and find out what menu items they like and dislike, or track your sales to give you this information. Find out why customers buy from you and not the competition down the road. If they tell you they love you because yours is a local business, then promote this in every facet of your advertising. If they tell you they love your coffee, then be sure to promote your delicious brew. If you discover your customers need a meeting room and you have the space, add one. To be successful, you will need to understand your customers, care about them and do all you can to fulfill their needs. The relationship is a bit like a marriage. You want a committed relationship and to attain it, you have to go the extra mile. When you've won real loyalty, even if you make a huge mistake, your customers know you and will hang in there.

Smart retail businesses have learned that a greeting and recognition work wonders.

In Japan the art of customer care is highly developed. A greeter bows to each person entering a department store and asks if she can be of assistance. The customer is always the honored guest. You don't have to hire a lady in a kimono but if your employees give every customer a friendly, welcoming greeting each time, your coffee bar will stand out in their minds. No matter how busy you are, acknowledge every customer. Make eye contact, smile and say a few words of welcome. Smart retail businesses have learned that a greeting and recognition work wonders.

Hire people-sensitive employees then train them well. See Chapters 6 and 7 for more on employees. You could have them practice various scripts, but by all means don't allow them to become robots, spouting the same insincere and boring phrases every time. But do require them to ask questions and talk to your customers. "Is this your first time here? Have you taken a look at our specials? Did you know we now have a catering service? We have hot muffins just out of the oven. Would you like to try one? Did you know all our coffees are certified organic?"

Help employees develop skills at reading gestures and body language and noticing when people seem interested in a teapot or the pastries. And yet, be sensitive about overwhelming customers, either with too much information or too much talk. Learn to recognize the confused new customer who is not sure how things work, and treat that person with total respect and patience.

Customer needs never end. What people want is individual dialog that changes with each interaction, so keep your antennae tuned to the competition and to signals from those who walk in your door. They usually have other coffeehouse options and don't need you. But you need them to survive. Ask yourself the toughest questions about your business performance. What basic wants and desires can you satisfy even better? What aesthetic and sensual delight can you offer that others don't? Only very high satisfaction will keep people coming back as loyal regulars.

Trust builds your income as loyal customers provide free word of mouth advertising. When people can totally count on you to create a marvelous experience every time, they will send their friends and bring their guests. As a general rule of marketing, keeping old customers costs you about one fifth as much as replacing dissatisfied people with new ones among the thousands of potentials out there. Rewarding regulars with an exceptional experience is the key to your success.

Narrow Your Marketing

You can't sell to everyone. The type of operation you open will help you decide which customers to target. Let's look at four examples and compare and contrast the similarities and differences in marketing each of them — a coffee drive-thru, a neighborhood coffeehouse, a kiosk in an office building and a coffee bar in a busy downtown area. In each example we will take for granted that customer service and drink quality are perfect.

> ...be sensitive about overwhelming customers, either with too much information or too much talk.

Drive-thru

Your customer at a drive-thru will more than likely be a commuter in a hurry. Convenience is the main reason people will patronize your business. Train your staff to serve customers quickly, and then promote speed in your marketing. In a drive-thru operation you won't be able to offer as large a menu as you would in a large, sit-down café. One chain Bellissimo worked with developed a concept that combined an outdoor drive-thru window with an inside walk-up counter. Their goal was to serve all customers in less than one minute.

You'll need to modify some of the techniques found in this book for marketing a drive-thru operation, but no matter what type of operation you decide to open, you must understand the needs of your customers. Study the local demographic and be smart enough to situate your drive-thru on a road that attracts early morning commuters and others who travel past throughout the day.

The Neighborhood Coffeehouse

As mentioned earlier, the small neighborhood café often becomes more important to the community than the products it sells. It becomes a place to read the paper and meet friends, in sociological terms "the third place," not your home and not your workplace. If your goal is to create a "third place" in your community, do all you can to make your interior warm and friendly and then encourage your customers to relax and spend time.

Provide enough seating so customers don't feel rushed or hurried because others are waiting to sit down. Provide outdoor seating where people can enjoy the sunshine, or can smoke. In his seminal book on design of spaces, *A Pattern Language*, architect Christopher Alexander strongly recommends that to encourage social interactions you provide movable tables and chairs. That allows people to expand a group as others arrive to join them. Or a couple can move away for an intimate conversation.

I have a close friend in the Midwest whose operation is the third place in her neighborhood. When I observed her operation, I discovered that most of her customers came because they felt welcome, safe and like a part of a family. She had wonderful roasted beans and her drinks were excellent, but her biggest marketing advantage was a reputation as a local meeting place.

Chains have recently begun moving into her area, and in a future chapter I will discuss how she marketed against them. But she has something a cookie-cutter chain will never have — "local flavor!" No matter how deep a chain's pockets, they will never to able to compete with her on the mainstay of her marketing plan.

Cart or Kiosk Operations in an Office Building or Hospital

I have also owned this type of business and it is without a doubt the easiest of the four examples to market, though you must limit your menu because of space constraints. It's easy to learn what businesses are around you and what types of people work in or visit your particular building. If your cart or kiosk is located in a high-risew in downtown Phoenix, and attorneys occupy most of the offices, you may want to market differently than you would if your operation was in a suburban hospital in Minneapolis.

In a hospital, it's easy to include coupons in the weekly employee newsletter or to visit each department and hand them out. It's also easy to drop off menus in each and every break room. In this type of operation you have a captive clientele. Many small operations in hospitals give specialty drinks a catchy marketing name. You could call a triple shot of espresso "The Defibrillator." Silly, but quite effective. A shop in a hospital may want to keep long hours. If the operation is in an office building, you may be open from early morning and choose to leave at four or five p.m., five days a week, giving you evenings and weekends to concentrate more management time on marketing your business.

The Downtown Big City Coffee Bar

If you open your operation in midtown Manhattan, or the financial heart of any large city, you will quickly realize that most of your clients have limited time. You must teach your employees to chat less and give great customer service with tremendous speed. Your menu should reflect what the rushed urban sophisticate wants. You may want to install an overhead television and play a financial channel or CNN.

No matter what type of operation you have and no matter where it is located, do your homework before you plan and develop any marketing plan. The more information you have about your customers, the better you can serve them and the more effective your marketing plan will be.

Chapter 4

Marketing Your Menu

Your menu is one of the most important aspects of your business. You will maximize your chances for success if you dedicate plenty of time and thought to planning and developing the perfect menu for your particular location, concept and clientele.

Your goal is to find and present the ideal food and beverage mix for your location and your customers. The type of operation you choose, cost restraints, and space limitations are factors you'll need to consider when developing your menu.

Everything you do in planning your business should start with your menu, including your store design. How can you expand your menu unless you have room for the needed equipment to prepare the items? Suppose you are already open and decide to add panini to your menu. Can you find space to put the panini press and sandwich prep area in your existing configuration?

Today, a coffee bar is much more than a coffee bar and in most cases you must sell much more than just coffee.

Times Change

A decade ago, on a scale of one to ten, I would have given a value of three to the importance of your coffeehouse menu. At that time, most coffee operations sold only espresso drinks and pastries. Today, things are quite different, and I would give menu development a nine on the same scale. With far more competition out there, customers may choose your operation over another because you have a more varied menu and you market your menu offerings to them in a unique manner.

Clients often tell me they want to offer a simple and extremely limited menu in a very large café. Some consultants will tell you this is a good idea, preaching this ten-year-old mantra to make their job easier. They develop a simple cookie-cutter menu and tell you it will work anywhere. Nothing could be farther from the truth.

Today, a coffee bar is much more than a coffee bar and in most cases you must sell much more than just coffee if you want to be successful. If you have an existing operation, don't be afraid to tweak, change and update your menu. It would be foolish and disastrous not to. Of course, you will test every recipe, calculate costs to the penny, and test your employees' ability to perfectly make each item on your menu every time.

Two Clients

On the day we met, one client told me that he would never consider serving anything but coffee and morning pastries — period. While searching for a location for his business, we spoke to over 50 coffee retailers as we traveled the state. Everywhere we went, we heard the same story. You need to serve more than coffee and pastries to make a profit in this business. My client soon changed his mind and we developed a full menu for his operation. He said a few years later, "Thank goodness I listened to you and the other retailers we talked to. I would be broke and out of business if I had gone with that simple menu I had originally planned."

I had another bullheaded client on the East Coast who had developed his menu long before he contacted Bellissimo. I had to fight tooth and nail to get him to consider my input on his menu. I'm happy to report I won the battle. He did listen, but with a lot of skepticism. During the first week of operation, he was averaging $1500 a day in sales. Over half of these sales came from items he had not originally wanted as part of his menu mix.

A Decade of Change in America

Twelve years ago there were hundreds of coffee operations in Seattle, and approximately 90 percent of them served very a limited menu. Today, most of these operations are either gone or serve expanded menu offerings. Why? As we discussed in Chapter 3, you must give your customers what they want. If you are operating in a newer market, learn from Seattle's coffee history. The only real history in the U.S. specialty coffee industry comes from Seattle, Portland and San Francisco. Over the years, coffee businesses in these cities have adapted to the needs of their customers. To be successful, learn the importance of the menu from these pioneering retailers.

A Century of Italian Coffee

My father grew up in a small village in Italy, and he frequently mentioned the "bar place" he went to almost every day. There, only men gathered to gossip and have coffee or a drink. Italy has a much longer coffee history than the U.S, so let's take a look at the evolution of the coffee bar menu in that country.

Some years ago, I met with the vice president of a large company in Northern Italy. Over lunch he told me how the coffee industry had changed in his country over the past 50 years. Coffee retailers realized they were catering to less than half the population. To market to the others, women and children, they began to incorporate items such as panini, gelato (Italian ice cream), fruit-flavored granita and other snacks into their menus.

If you visit almost any modern coffee operation in Italy today, you'll usually find a very diverse menu. Many upscale operations have beautiful glass displays of gourmet chocolate and in the more trendy and tourist operations you'll usually find a large gift section. Times have changed in this business. You and your operation must change with them, just as Northwest and Italian coffee operations have.

If you visit almost any modern coffee operation in Italy today, you'll usually find a very diverse menu.

Coffee is the Hook

No matter how extensive your menu is, your business is first and foremost a coffee operation. Your primary identity is your coffee. You want to be known as THE coffee operation in your area, the one that serves the very best coffee. To do this, you must fully understand the nuances of your product. That is a tall order, and requires you to fully educate yourself. Few start-up coffeehouse owners have done this. The result is that purists and knowledgeable afficionados could feel ripped off and resort to home brewing.

With their history, Italians know how to make a great cappuccino. A true cappuccino, like other espresso drinks, combines skillfully roasted coffee beans, perfectly extracted espresso and carefully steamed milk, not to mention the craftsmanship of a talented barista. With the shot or shots of espresso already in the cup, the milk is poured in. The result is the wonderful wet beverage that is like a dessert.

Before I became involved with this business I wondered why a cappuccino was bitter coffee with large, dry bubbles in America, but so smooth and pleasurable in Europe. In the early 90s, the best coffee roasters in Seattle were using age-old Italian techniques and blending to achieve proper taste. But at that time many American roasters burned their beans, totally over-roasting in the search for an espresso strong enough to hold up in milk-based drinks.

So was that the whole problem? Not quite. Even with Seattle's best roasted beans, in the early 90s you could almost bet the steaming and texturizing of the milk would be bastardized and shots would be improperly pulled. Drinks are getting better, but if an operation does not follow certain non-arguable standards a cappuccino will never taste the way it should. So many variables lead us to the perfection of the "true cappuccino."

Beans must be properly roasted and blended to withstand the rigors of a professional machine. The grind must be set so that the coffee does not extract too quickly or too slowly. A proper pack or tamp in the portafilter is also necessary for the optimum 20- to 25-second extraction. Milk frothing, steaming and texturizing is a learned art. The person preparing the beverage must be careful at each stage of the heating process to ensure rich, wet, creamy foam. Milk is generally expanded only until the temperature reaches about 90 degrees (Fahrenheit). At this point, the goal is not further expansion, but texture of the milk, which should never be heated to above 140 - 145 degrees.

I welcome the day when I can order a cappuccino without being disappointed. When the public is more educated people will demand higher quality. Great drink preparation is certainly not brain surgery. It's only learning certain fundamentals and applying these to each and every drink served.

If you decide not to roast, buy the best beans, even if they're the most expensive. (We will go into great detail about this in Chapter 8, *Selling the Beans*.) Then, train your staff to prepare them perfectly. Base your reputation on quality. If your customers believe your coffee is the very best, it's easier to convince your customers that your selections of teas and other products are also the best. Don't ever let them down.

The person preparing the beverage must be careful at each stage of the heating process to ensure rich, wet, creamy foam.

Your Visual Menu
With your computer, you can produce clear, simple and legible point-of-sale signs to put on the counter and in display cases. But hire a graphics professional to create the larger signs outside and inside your business, including your large menu boards. Make your menu easy to understand, easy to read and not too cluttered or complex. Put your food menu near your drink menu, where it's easy to see and may prompt an impulse buy.

Give items original names. But don't get too cute. Foreign words, not translated, can put people off. If you offer a Bangkok Panini, explain what it is or you'll leave customers baffled. Study the menus of other coffeehouses. Read the menus of successful upscale restaurant chains for inspiration and creativity.

> Try products from more than one company and, if the product looks promising, customer input will help you decide which to choose.

If you're in a fast-paced business district, distribute menus with your phone number and Web address. Let people phone in orders and pick them up with no waiting. Your menu should be both descriptive and alluring.

Marketing the Perfect Menu

Once you've developed the perfect menu of offerings, you can market these in-store to increase sales and emphasize your unique and excellent products. Use proven methods to encourage customers to try new items.

Sampling

Sampling works in two different situations. First, if you're considering selling a new product but aren't sure if your customers will buy it, sampling will allow you to find out if your customers are even interested in the product. Use small sample cups and let them try it. Suppliers will usually provide free samples of a product if you express interest in selling it. Try products from more than one company and, if the product looks promising, customer input will help you decide which to choose.

Second, use sampling if you've introduced a great item and want to encourage customers to start buying it. By giving away samples of the item, you can quickly double your sales. I had a client who opened an operation in a resort island community. He had three colorful heads of granita spinning before his customers' eyes, but no one was ordering it. We decided to offer customers a small taste of the product. Within two days, my client was selling more than 50 granita drinks a day.

Serve a Coffee of the Day/Week/Month

In addition to your normal house blend, promote an origin coffee on a daily, weekly or monthly basis. Advertise this special coffee with distinctive signs. "Bellissimo Clip Art: Countries of Origin" works well for producing these yourself. If, for example, your coffee of the week is Guatemalan Antigua, use your computer to generate a large sign with a colorful image of Guatemala and place it near your ordering station. Text on the sign could read, "Try our recently arrived Guatemalan beans from Antigua, shade-grown and eco-friendly. This rich coffee is available all month, by the cup and on sale by the pound at $2 off our regular price."

Create Drink Specials with Unique Names

One of the most important marketing tactics you can implement won't cost you a dime. The *Wall Street Journal* reported that a large American coffee company attributed part of its growth to the practice of creating a "new" beverage almost every quarter. All that was really new was the name. Even a small individual coffee bar can offer a new drink and promote it each week. This may appear a bit too aggressive, but one of the marketing advantages of being small is your ability to change without navigating through a huge bureaucracy.

Every independent coffee retailer should have a unique specialty drink menu. A coffee bar that Bellissimo opened in Los Angeles served nothing but Hawaiian coffee and called the specialty lattes "Kona Sunset" and "Hang Ten." Smoothies on the menu included "Island Mango Madness." A retailer in Texas offered the "Six-Shooter" and the "Branding Iron." Tourists loved the names and so did the locals. When I opened my first coffee bar, I named all of my specialty drinks after towns in Italy, in keeping with my Italian theme.

> **Every independent coffee retailer should have a unique specialty drink menu.**

Table Tents

You can announce your latest drinks with simple acrylic table tents. Change these advertisements weekly or monthly. As a small retailer, you could create a drink called the "Patriot Latte" for the Fourth of July, or use eggnog instead of milk during the holidays. Advertise these special "limited time" drinks right on your tables.

What about Decaf?

Recent marketing research showed that 63 percent of specialty coffee drinkers ordered decaffeinated drinks at least part of the time. Surprised? Times are changing. The prejudice against decaffeinated coffee goes back to a belief it offers inferior taste. Since 1997, the Swiss Water process has been vastly improved and the flavors are much richer. Most respondents to a recent questionnaire said decaf tastes similar to regular coffee.

The typical coffeehouse dedicates less than a quarter of its coffee menu space to decaf drinks. Decaf drinkers tend to be more health-conscious than the average person. A certified organic, Swiss Water process decaffeinated coffee is the logical choice to appeal to these customers.

Create a More Diverse Menu
Most hot coffee is sold before ten in the morning. You plan to be open all day. Do you have a strategy for profits during all hours? Be creative with unique breakfast ideas. Bagels, granola, yogurt, fresh fruit or frozen waffles might work for you. A soup and sandwich menu for mid-day, plus iced coffee, smoothies and granita for afternoon can keep people buying. In the warm months add ice cream or gelato.

Ten years ago, few if any coffee bars in America had panini or gelato on the menu. Today, most coffee bars Bellissimo opens serve panini, and many also serve gelato. A diverse menu will create more reasons for customers to visit your business. If your morning coffee business stops at eleven, light lunch items like panini can attract a lunchtime crowd. You can use a panini grill to heat bagels and sandwiches too. During afternoon and evening hours, the sale of gelato will add additional dollars to your register.

Add interest to your menu with an excellent presentation of each item you prepare. How about a classy wafer flavored with exotic syrup served on a saucer with each order of espresso? Colorful or oddball straws, toppings of colored sugars, a bit of powdered sugar on a chocolate tart or a tiny cookie on a frozen treat all add to the artistic effect and impress customers with your intent to add something extra.

Use your imagination. One of your big advantages as an independent operator is that no one will stop you from trying creative ideas. You can test and experiment, and find out what people like. Appeal to local loyalties, honoring your home team, famous hometown people, memorable nearby places and important events. Listen to the feedback. Use your advantage as a small business owner to build a menu that sets you apart. An excellent menu is crucial to your success, as is your ability to market your offerings in unique and creative ways.

Set the Right Prices

Since you are selling a great experience and the highest possible quality, avoid the temptation to compete with lower prices. In this business, it just won't work. Number one, you can't afford it. For one thing, your costs are higher because you can never buy in the quantities a huge corporation can.

So how do you set prices? If you buy ready items like bagels or yogurt, normally you can make a fair profit if you double the wholesale price. If your staff prepares items from scratch, figure the precise cost of ingredients and multiply by four. If this rule leads to a price too high to sell, you may choose to take a small loss or to accept the fact that you can't afford to offer this item.

To understand more about pricing, look carefully at numbers. Assuming both items take the same amount of employee time to prepare, you can make a higher percent of profit on a cup of tea that costs you 18 cents and sells for $1.25. But you may make more money on a granita with a dollar cost that sells for three dollars. To understand your full costs, look at the resources each menu item demands, the space, the equipment and the preparation time. Set your opening prices just slightly lower than the largest chain store. Research shows that people perceive value in products, yet shop prices.

> **Use your advantage as a small business owner to build a menu that sets you apart.**

The bottom line is this: No matter how good your menu, you will still need to use creative marketing techniques to sell it. Take a hint from Madison Avenue and create sizzle and excitement around your products. Increased sales are sure to follow.

Chapter 5

Everything Must be Perfect

Though we all know achieving perfection is impossible, clearly it's in the best interest of your business to strive for it. The goal of success demands that you seek perfection in every area discussed in this book. Any one of them can make or break your operation.

Perfection from the First

Much of the consulting that Bellissimo does is "damage control," when people hire our company after their businesses are open and ask us how they can make them more profitable. This type of consulting job is without a doubt the most difficult.

> **Shape and temper, add and subtract, juggle and rethink, until the fit is perfect and the design is unique.**

It's much easier to do things right the first time. To motivate employees with lackluster attitudes and improper training, or to correct poor store design after the fact, is a tremendous challenge. I've been in situations where I've told an owner I would fire all but one of his employees and I've seen stores so poorly designed that, without spending $10,000 to $20,000, not much could be done to correct the deficiencies.

If you're reading this book and haven't built-out your coffee bar, make sure you hire professionals to help you create a location that is as perfect as possible from the outset. You may have brilliant ideas and be eager to start, but wait. Talk to commercial kitchen experts, restaurant designers, architects, decorators, signage artists, color consultants, and more. Observe what other successful operations are doing. Read all you can. Shape and temper, add and subtract, juggle and rethink, until the fit is perfect and the design is unique.

If you're already open, read marketing books to improve on what you have but, if you are implementing new ideas, do them right the first time. Then, market as if the life of your business depends on it, because it does!

Perfection in Every Area

U.S. Army advertisers coined the phrase, "Be the best that you can be." As corny as that may sound, it's essential for your business to be all it can be, too. Of course, you'll make mistakes. The best and the brightest do. I met a successful businessman who told me that he felt only 30 percent of his ideas were good ones. He believed that was a great percentage. Another wealthy entrepreneur said that for every ten business ideas that excited him, after doing the research, only one turned out to be worth an investment.

Pitchers who win 65 percent of their games are all stars. If you could hit a home run once in every three at-bats, you would definitely be a marketing all star and end up in the business hall of fame. Strive for a homerun every time, but be realistic. Accept what happens, learn from your errors and continue to give 100 percent to your business.

Although no person or business is perfect, the most successful strive for perfection in every area. Many settle for less, so your efforts to be the best will put you in the lead and make your business unique. With so much mediocrity in today's world, those who try hard and go the extra mile will be recognized and rewarded.

As time passes and more and more consolidation takes place in this industry, you'll find yourself marketing against large chains that employ people who spend their days focused on beating the competition through good marketing. But you can stay savvy, learn from them and often outwit them. Watch what they do then add the perfect twist that fits your operation and location.

Perfect Product

The perfect cup starts with the best available beans. But don't assume every customer can appreciate the finest beans without a little guidance. Part of good marketing includes giving people background and information about coffee, usually available from your suppliers. Let your customers know if you roast your own, or buy from an award-winning roaster. Display roasting dates prominently. A big part of education is learning to discern differences. When you educate the consumer, you build sophistication and a willingness to pay a premium price.

> A big part of education is learning to discern differences.

Recently, during a week of travel in Colorado, I found only one nearly perfect espresso, from a barista in Steamboat Springs. I was shocked, not because the search was so long, but because I found even one. I've often said espresso is misunderstood in the U.S. On a trip through Italy, I consumed over 60 espresso beverages, and 55 were absolutely perfect. American retailers don't come close to this now, but they must learn and aim for perfection. Coffee is getting better and yours must also, to survive the onslaught of competition.

One reason coffeehouses can get away with inferior product is that many consumers still don't understand the nuances of great coffee. We can still camouflage our bad preparation with too much milk and sweet, flavored syrups. When we do this, we waste the potential of hand-picked and carefully sorted beans from the far reaches of the globe. This seems unconscionable to me. Education about the product is key to making the perfect beverage truly appreciated.

Our customers, the coffee lovers, will continue to become more knowledgeable every year. For our industry to continue to grow, we must serve truly excellent coffee drinks. I want to encourage small independent retailers to admit they could learn more, try harder and become more innovative. To do well, you have to do it right. Strive for perfection in your entire operation, beginning with every cup you serve. It's the key to survival and growth.

The Perfect Procedures

The successful operation requires excellent systems. The systems you develop for training your employees may be the most important part of what you do behind the scenes in your specialty coffee business. If your employees can't prepare and serve a perfect product, you are missing the point of opening a coffeehouse — to impact the community with quality coffee and to gain recognition for it.

In Italy, the coffee business has come up with what they call the four Ms of the perfect espresso beverage.

Macinazione, or machining, refers to the perfect grinding of the coffee, which will vary even with the weather. For each cup, the seven to eight grams of coffee, as fine as sugar, must never be ground too far in advance or your coffee will lose freshness and its potential.

Miscela is mixing, the perfect blending of the coffee for a complex and harmonious flavor. Most Italian coffeehouses add robusta beans to the usual arabica, providing more caffeine and a denser "crema."

Macchina refers to the perfect espresso machine, one that is always immaculately cared for. The right commercial machine will produce nine atmospheres of pressure to force water through the finest grind and extract essential oils, which carry the flavors to the cup.

Mano refers to the skilled hand, the manual labor contributed by the barista of passion and experience. The barista is the most important of the four Ms, the artist who holds the brush.

The Perfect Place

Let's assume your business is beautifully decorated, full of impressive innovations and has an excellent ambiance. It's graced with elegant lighting and plush with scrumptious color and texture. The floors are fascinating, the tables unique, the seating comfortable. The equipment gleams, the counters are wiped constantly. Even the restrooms get hourly attention. Congratulations. You are now doing only the minimum.

Every inch of your business must be sparkling clean at all times. People may not consciously notice your cleaning efforts unless you fall below their personal standards, but they will sense some trustworthy quality they can't name in a clean, uncluttered location. Inspect the place yourself as often as possible. Note any improvements needed and be sure they are implemented. Assign someone to constantly patrol the seating area — bussing cups, washing tables and hard chairs, whisking away papers and debris, straightening furniture, sweeping and keeping glass surfaces spotless. Then and only then will you have achieved the nuances of perfection.

The Perfect Welcome

Greet everyone who walks in your door. You want your customers to remember a smiling face and an enthusiastic welcome that makes them feel special. Make eye contact. Let them know you're glad to see them. When your staff is upbeat and eager to serve, customers feel as if they are among friends. They will happily spend money, tell their friends about your unique place, and return often. Observe your employees constantly and make constructive suggestions about acknowledging customers.

Perfect Solutions to Problems

Are you in the habit of hiding errors or glossing over bad experiences? Do you deal with humiliation or stupidity by pretending it never happened? Or do you take the opposite tack, and blow up, shaming your employees until they wish they could quit?

Be positive. Mistakes are not crimes, only feedback from the universe. Look at those embarrassing moments as free advice and totally objective pointers. They direct wise business owners to change how they think and point to ways to tweak their operation. Welcome the opportunity to fix what doesn't quite work, and to improve your employee training. The biggest mistake is to learn nothing from an error, which guarantees that it will happen again.

The biggest mistake is to learn nothing from an error, which guarantees that it will happen again.

No matter how good you are, you'll occasionally get a complaint. Though some people love to gripe, most complaints are justified. The best response to a person poised for an argument is to agree and to sympathize. "You're right, of course. I'm so sorry this happened to you. We want you to be one 100 percent satisfied, every time you visit us. Let me take care of it right now."

Some employees may insist on a logical excuse for why the unfortunate incident happened. But whose fault it is, is of no interest to the unhappy patron. The upset customer wants action now, not someone shifting the blame. An instant and friendly response is your best defense. Empower employees to correct most problems immediately without seeking management approval.

Unconditional customer satisfaction is your goal, and though it may occasionally cost you a few pennies, salvaging a bad moment with grace and goodwill goes a long way toward creating loyalty. If the customer says the coffee is not perfect, your employees need to know they can offer a choice of any beverage free, as compensation. A quick and sincere response will surprise and disarm even hostile guests. You can turn an error into an opportunity when you turn a mistake around, and create a relationship.

You want an unhappy customer to know you really care and regret what happened. Follow up and ask if they were happy with the solution. Or you can create customer comment cards, preaddressed to you. This provides a direct route to management if people have strong emotions. Instruct employees to fill out daily reports on any problems, how it happened and how they resolved it. The only stigma or negative result should come from not learning from an unpleasant experience or incident.

Provide Perfect Leadership

The small business owner and manager has a job millions yearn for, with a chance to inspire others and to turn a vision into a profitable reality. In your own coffee shop, your leadership skills can grow and serve you well if you accept full accountability for the outcome of your actions and those of everyone who works for you.

The great leader, be it manager or owner, lives a life of purpose with clear long-term goals. With a positive outlook, the sky is the limit. Define your large and small goals. List obstacles and chores, research to be done, expertise to be found, then set up timelines as part of a fully developed plan that includes a way to measure your success. Then get to work. With daily and weekly goal setting, you can modify a mediocre operation into one that is nearly perfect.

To lead and manage on a day-to-day basis, in your coffeehouse, you have to plan and stay organized so you can provide direction as to who will do what, when, and how. Each employee needs to know what you expect and what is not permitted. You earn respect by displaying your own passion and skills, and by inspiring people to learn from you and to set personal goals.

Define your large and small goals. List obstacles and chores, research to be done, expertise to be found.

As a leader with good people skills, you can attract and keep talented employees who are committed to your goals. To lead effectively, you must see past your own wants to understand why people do what they do and to understand and accept human failure. Use your imagination to see reality from their point of view. Employees know when you have their best interests in mind. An excellent manager sincerely wants others to do well and seeks to motivate them to unlock their own potential.

The good leader thinks carefully before speaking, like a diplomat, but also will use body language and visual clues that add meaning. Educators talk about seven different brain types, each with its own way of learning. Some people will not get it when you tell them, but need to try it themselves to get a feel for it. Others won't make sense of a written explanation but will understand instantly when they see it done. For others the rhythm of practice will prove successful.

The good manager works to create a team with common goals of excellence. But select those goals to reflect true priorities, those that will make the biggest difference with the least effort. Train your people well and make sure they know what you expect each team member to do.

Your personal will and attitude set the tone for your entire operation.

Always set high standards and then put in place ways to measure how they are achieved. The best manager sets targets but does not micromanage how people go about achieving them. Show trust and encourage thinking by expecting employees to deal with the normal, everyday issues themselves.

Keep precise records. Make generous notes on everything that happens, and record incidents, as you just won't recall details later. Our top executives keep daily diaries noting everyone they talk with and what was said. Refer to your notes later, as needed. They could one day protect you from a lawsuit.

Always let people know when you like what you see. "Sabena, it's great the way you make eye contact with everyone." Reward excellence by telling the whole staff about achievements. "Jason sold 20 pounds of whole-bean coffee yesterday. That's a record." Pass on any compliments you hear. Positive reinforcement is powerful. Rarely criticize. If you see someone doing poorly, turn your disappointment into a teachable moment. Focus on the positive.

Your personal will and attitude set the tone for your entire operation. Good communication with customers and employees is basic to success. Don't stop there. Extend it to suppliers and other businesses you work with to expand your circle of goodwill and cooperation. It all starts with valuing and caring about others.

Always strive to create a winning team aiming for perfection. Strive to lead your staff by example, and always give 100 percent.

CHAPTER 6

HIRE AND KEEP GREAT EMPLOYEES

The Face of Your Business

From a marketing standpoint, no component of your business has more face-to-face impact than do the employees. The coffee business is unique. Your employee may be the first person a customer talks to in the morning, or the one they look forward to chatting with on a break from a hectic day. A coffeehouse is sexy and glamorous, unlike a visit to the dry cleaner. And because great coffee in a great setting is one of life's small yet elegant pleasures, to be a success you must attract charismatic employees and instill passion.

Specialty coffee consumers are typically of higher income, intelligence, experience and expectation than the average. They are dissatisfied with what passes for service in many stores. They generally will not accept mediocrity as inevitable. They want more than a great cup of coffee or the best cinnamon roll in the city. They expect and seek a sincere effort to make them happy – in short, a humanizing retail experience. Your hiring decisions determine whether or not you can provide the products and service that keep your customers keep coming back.

> "I was not really buying coffee. It was the social interaction and the friendly faces I saw day after day that made me stop at Joe's place."

Customer Service is Marketing

For some time I have wanted to write a magazine article called "I Pay a Dollar a Day to Say Hello to Joe." On my way to work I usually stop at a little coffee bar and neighborhood hangout. Most mornings I have a five-minute conversation with Joe, the owner, about an upcoming football or basketball game, the weather or some controversial world event.

After a year, I began to wonder why I made this stop each morning and spent a dollar for a cup of brewed coffee. In another five minutes, I would arrive at my office where I had access to a $10,000 two-group espresso machine and some of the finest beans in the country. Was I crazy?

No. The reason is, I was not really buying coffee. It was the social interaction and the friendly faces I saw day after day that made me stop at Joe's place. I came to realize this camaraderie was worth a few dollars a week to me. My stop provided a social experience worth paying for because Joe and his employees understood the basic principles of customer service. Joe's coffee bar had become my third place.

Good customer service is the first step in good marketing. Most of the people who walk through your door or drive up to your window will expect your employees to be courteous, friendly and professional. They count on special treatment as much as they count on receiving the high-quality product you hand them when you take their money. Next to great coffee, the most important thing you have to sell is excellent service. The right employees sell a great experience that creates repeat customers who tell their friends.

So how do you know if you're providing excellent service? Your customers will let you know what they think about your employees. I owned an operation where I worked only on Saturdays. My regulars did not hesitate to mention an employee's poor attitude or any bad drinks they were served while I was not in the coffee bar. I was pleased to learn from these unsolicited reports that mistakes were few. I'd hired good people. You can too, if you know what you're looking for.

Hire Great People

When interviewing an applicant, look for style, intrinsic charm, intelligence and passion. When you interview, allow candidates to talk. Find out if the person actually likes coffee. Ask a little about his or her life. Is this a night or morning person? Ask questions that will showcase the candidate's personality.

What jobs have they had? It's great if they know the business already, but experience may be a big drawback if people have to unlearn bad habits. Anyone can be trained to make a perfect cappuccino. Attitude, personality and passion are difficult to change after childhood. People who respect themselves, love people, love coffee and are proud to work for you will add thousands to your bottom line each year.

I know from personal experience that one wrong person can bring down the whole staff. To attract a loyal local clientele, look for employees with an upbeat outlook and an eagerness to serve. You want every customer to feel that this visit they make to your café is important in your life. Neither they nor you will be satisfied with baristas who look at the job as a way to make a few extra bucks, and who couldn't care less about how they serve products or how customers perceive your business.

People who respect themselves, love people, love coffee and are proud to work for you will add thousands to your bottom line each year.

As many retail operations have learned, older workers can be great. Lots of healthy retired folks love to be out among people. Some may have been professionals and now want part-time work with fewer responsibilities. They can be slower to learn, but they have outgrown their egotism and are often highly dependable. Retired people can put in flexible hours and may turn out to be the bedrock of your staff, offering suggestions and giving emotional support to younger employees.

You can train people to perfect a certain skill set, but you'll rarely be able to change someone's ingrained attitude.

Socially adept people shine in a coffeehouse. Hire fun "people" people. They enhance everyone's morale, often a contagious condition. Treat them like friends, not underlings. Ask for their opinions. Keep them happy and they will show up and make work a pleasure. When staff spirits rise, profits also rise.

How many people do you need? Scheduling is a learned art form. Having enough people on the job is crucial to customer satisfaction. If a guest has to wait too long when her time is short, she will remember the experience with disgust. We've all been there — the post office at noon, three of the five windows closed and a line out the door. But it's almost as big a mistake to have too many people working. They get bored and move with little enthusiasm. The ideal is to schedule just enough workers to pre- serve a sense of hustle and a chance for up-selling. Staff members need enough time to interact with each guest and to do a good job of selling extras like beans or small wares.

The people you hire will make or break your operation. No matter how clever you are, if you don't hire the right employees to carry out your ideas, you have lost the battle before you have even begun to fight. Not every eager, attractive, capable person can do well in your business. When hiring, look for people who not only have the ability to prepare products with flair and perfection but who also have personality you want as the "face" of your business. You can train people to perfect a certain skill set, but you'll rarely be able to change someone's ingrained attitude.

The Right Person for the Job
From a technical standpoint it's difficult, but not as hard as some would have you believe, to become an excellent barista. However,

even though you may teach your employees the proper steps and nuances of coffee preparation, they might not possess the passion necessary to become the exceptional barista your customers will look forward to seeing every day.

Make sure you pair an employee with a job that suits his or her personality. The importance of the right person in the right job is illustrated by what happened at a drive-thru opening in a North Carolina town. The owner and I over-hired, knowing a few of the new employees wouldn't work out. Two workers in particular were having a difficult time working on the machine and preparing drinks. Our first thought was to let them go, since they did not appear to have the necessary skills to prepare drinks to our expectations.

But after watching them work for a week, we realized that each of them had a great personality at the window and was a fantastic salesperson. They remembered names, didn't forget to tell customers about specials and, best of all, they had warm and friendly smiles that brought people back day after day. Since we had employees who excelled as baristas, we rethought job descriptions. These two charmers only prepared beverages in a crisis situation. At the window, they were perfect cashiers and displayed an enthusiasm impossible for many of the better baristas.

Keep Good Employees

Your goal is to hire, train and retain great employees. It costs you time and effort to bring on new people and get them up to speed. To keep the employees who can think fast, solve problems and welcome every guest, you have to do more than just chose them with care. You must train them well and pay them fairly.

Your goal is to hire, train and retain great employees.

For a happy team, communication is key. Hold weekly or bi-monthly meetings and ask for staff opinions. Get any problems out in the open to halt gossip and work toward solutions. Be sure everyone feels safe enough to point out what YOU could do better. Listen to your employees — they are on the front line each and every day. You may be amazed by their marketing ideas and insights into areas of your business that you have overlooked. Be humble. In some cases they may know your business better than you do.

Nurture your staff as you do your profits. Build morale and loyalty with fringe benefits such as health care, bonuses for high performance, company retreats and profit sharing. If employees are not secure and happy, they will not produce their best. Give them the power to keep customers happy. Back them up on their crisis decisions when they adhere to store policy, even if you could have done better.

See your whole staff as a team, with you as the coach. Hold them to the highest standards and never back down on quality. Don't expect them to do what you won't do yourself. Praise them for good work. Treat them with respect and absolute fairness. Try hard not to show favoritism. Correct them in private, never in front of others, with the emphasis on understanding and learning more. Document serious infractions in your employee's file. In serious situations, have another present for meetings as a witness, and elevate the conversation from the "he said, she said" level.

Inform employees of your plans and discuss your options with them so they don't feel out of the loop. Give them ample warning about changes coming up. On a positive note, let them know about your business challenges and ask for input, then keep them informed of progress toward shared goals such as cost control or volume increase.

Staff look to you to keep their work environment sane and safe, even if they are only with you a few hours per week as part of a busy life. Problems don't fix themselves. It's your job to nip trouble in the bud. An activity that costs you money and customers, and any unacceptable behavior, needs to be stopped quickly. You're the one who pays if problems continue or grow.

Your guidance is essential to establish standards. Create a written employee manual with company policies and job descriptions. Every employee should get one at the time of hiring and be expected to read it. The manual provides policy to back you up when someone steps out of bounds. Have each employee sign and date a form stating that they have read and understood the manual. Put this document in their file. If you are like most managers, you will learn new lessons every month and these can be incorporated into your manual with regular updates. Have employees sign that they have read and understood the updates.

If you suspect you made a hiring mistake, first work on a solution with the individual and set a time limit for change. Stick to it — no backing down. You don't operate a charity. If things don't improve, check your state's laws, then fire him.

Never underestimate how important your employees are to your business — they are your business. A woman who tells customers colorful stories about estate coffee growers is a woman who brings in profits. A cashier who recalls 300 customer names is a treasure. A shy busboy who arrives on time and works steadily deserves your appreciation. A barista who strikes the ideal balance between knowledge and passion can create a beverage of unparalleled perfection and can make your coffeehouse famous.

Never underestimate how important your employees are to your business – they are your business.

Good people are the future of your business. It's the reason that, despite the poor service and the volume of mediocre espresso in the marketplace, people still look to the future of new coffee bars with anticipation. Someday, with your own passion and input, we may come close to the Italian view of this job as a valued profession, with every barista in touch with his espresso machine — like a Formula One driver with his car or a jazz musician with his horn. Your job in hiring is to locate individuals that display potential for this level of passion.

CHAPTER 7

TRAIN YOUR EMPLOYEES

Training for Perfection

Training may be the most important job for an owner or manager, and it's never-ending. Managers will tell you they train their employees, but usually they don't do enough of it to build respect for coffee and their customers. Turnover is rapid in food service, so a structured program is essential. Your employees will learn and practice excellence only if YOU make sure they get the training they need. If you have six or more employees, you may want to appoint your oldest, most knowledgeable or most stable person as a training director.

Your dreams of success will simply not be realized if your people don't get the best possible training. The initial training of a new staff person is without a doubt one of the most important factors in marketing your business. And frequent refreshers will prove important. Sometimes overwhelmed when first hired, people may pick up bad habits when unable to retain the volumes of detail in all they were told. Your marketing program, no matter how good it is, can't overcome mistakes that are inevitable unless staff members have a regimen of highly structured basic training, then receive regular updates on their coffeehouse education.

Share information with your staff. Post any interesting educational materials and pertinent articles or make copies to send home. Hundreds of books cover various parts of the industry. Contact the Specialty Coffee Association of America for catalogs. Bellissimo (www.espresso101.com) has dozens of materials including books, CD-ROMs, DVDs and videos that will take your employees step-by-step through drink preparation techniques. Let employees take these home. Afterwards, challenge them with tough questions and testing, both written and hands-on.

Talk about quality and high standards at every staff meeting. Be sure your employees understand you want to be the best and expect them to be proud of working for you. Let them know it's better to waste a drink than to serve one that is not correct. Hold regular sessions to review and improve employee skills. Let your people know about outside training opportunities.

To produce an exceptional, cutting-edge barista, the key is passion. Your training must cultivate passion and a penchant for quality in your students. They will either have passion or they won't. Baristas will either care deeply about coffee and your operation or they will look at their job as simply a way of making money. With your experience, you should be able to quickly observe where they stand.

The two big parts of training are customer relations and technical skills. Technical skills are crucial, and they can be learned. Making great coffee is an art form, no matter how fine the beans and the machines. A poor drink is the result of poor training.

But technical skill is not the whole story. Light a fire in any employee who shows an eagerness to learn how to prepare the perfect cup of coffee. If you can do this, then the rest is easy. When your employees take pride in the drinks they serve, they will want to share their enthusiasm with your customers.

In my two magazine articles about baristas, "The Italian Barista" and "The American Barista," I interviewed people who really loved their jobs. I wrote the American piece four or five years after the Italian story, and was encouraged to find that American baristas were as enthusiastic as their Italian counterparts. Many wanted to make coffee a career.

A memorable barista from Minneapolis waxed poetic for 15 minutes, proudly telling me how perfect her café's beans were and how people would travel up to 30 miles just to buy them. Others, she said, would go miles out of their way to visit the café for a perfectly prepared cappuccino. She'd had numerous jobs since college, but when she started working for her present employer she knew she had found something more valuable than trading her time for money — she had found an employer whose ideals were similar to her own.

As an owner you want employees who think like you do and have the same vested interest in doing well, employees who are proud to represent your dream. How do you achieve that goal? First, screen your job candidates well and then implement a stringent training program.

When your employees take pride in the drinks they serve, they will want to share their enthusiasm with your customers.

A client of mine who owned an operation in New England covered for an employee of hers who prepared me a mediocre latte. She said, "Serena is new and I haven't spent the proper training time with her yet. I really need to make time soon." I found that frightening. How many bad drinks will this employee serve before she is properly trained? There's just no excuse for poor training. How many new or regular customers will be turned off by an inferior drink, and go elsewhere? The answer is probably hundreds.

Be a Great Teacher

Before you can be a teacher, you must spend serious time as a student yourself. Sad to say, many coffeehouse owners don't know as much as they should. Surveying the competition, for one of my clients, I walked into a coffee bar where the owner had just spent about a quarter million to create a beautiful store. I said, "Can I have a single espresso...and could you pull the shot very short, please." After 20 seconds the young woman replied, "I'm sorry, but we aren't allowed to do that. It's store policy." She looked terrified.

Soon the manager appeared and I explained what I wanted. He said, "The machine is calibrated to pull a shot of espresso only one way and I can't change its programming." I asked if I could watch and have them pull the demitasse out early. "No, store policy."

I had been nice up to this point but I just couldn't hold back. I said, "I'm sorry. I'm not sure what came over me. I thought I was your customer." I went on to explain that this policy and lack of understanding of the product itself was beyond belief. The point of this story is that many owners and managers have a total lack of understanding of the product they serve, a serious problem for them that is easily remedied by education and proper training. Be sure you give yourself an in-depth education about your product — coffee.

Community colleges, management seminars, business magazines, trade shows, professional organizations, books, videos, DVDs and more exist to help you learn and succeed. Now, assuming you've done your own homework, we can talk about you as teacher.

What makes a good trainer? The same rules apply to the trainer as to the student. But trainers must have even more passion and must study and continue to learn from those who know more than they do. The key to becoming a knowledgeable trainer is reading books, asking questions and spending time with those who have been in the business for some time. Add to that a sincere desire to help others grow and learn, and your students will look forward to time spent learning with you.

There's more to great teaching than intellectual knowledge. You will demonstrate the simplest routine chore and the most complex process. You can describe the subtle differences in coffees and explain why you like what you drink. You don't want to exude snobbery, just love and familiarity with the nuances of the product. And you don't want to pretend brilliance by making coffee sound as difficult as quantum physics. Simplify and clarify everything, adding details as the student gains confidence.

Unfortunately, too many trainers are improperly trained and pass on their inferior skills to their students. If you find yourself in a time crunch, or experiencing a large turnover rate, then train a trainer to your own high standards. Someone must fully train employees before they serve even one drink to one customer, and then must keep them sharp.

The Perfect Drink

Don't underestimate the value that perfect drinks will create for your operation. A full understanding of this idea alone may be enough to set you apart. The books, videos and DVDs from Bellissimo go into the importance of the why and how to consistently create a perfect drink that you can be proud to serve. In this book, we won't discuss the ways to achieve perfect drinks, but will emphasize how important it is to your marketing success that every drink be perfect.

> Unfortunately, too many trainers are improperly trained and pass on their inferior skills to their students.

Teach Them What to Do and Say

Have your employees greet people as they walk in the door. Practice scripts until it becomes natural. Emphasize the importance of making eye contact, even if you can't serve them at once. People don't mind waiting if they know they have been seen and recognized. Call regulars by their first names.

For each beverage, some essential questions are — for here or to go, what kind, what size. Ask if they want it iced, hot or blended. For tea, ask if they want the tea bag on the side or in the hot water.

Ask the essential questions, and suggest something additional. If a customer is confused or hesitant, suggest they take a minute to study the posted menu. Offer help in the explanation of any products a customer may seem confused about.

If possible, to avoid chaos and confusion, take all orders at the cash register, where you can ring them up at once. If a customer is waiting in another place, ask them to come to you. "Hi, I can help you here." Or put up a sign over the order point that says, "Order here." Let customers figure out who was first if there's any uncertainty.

With friendliness, the order is taken and rung up. Institute a policy of always giving the customer the receipt. Instruct employees that failure to do so could lead to dismissal.

For each food item, have equal-sized portions already cut and a clean serving tool along side. Ask if they'd like a pastry. Prepare the order, serving it correctly. After heating, add to the side of the plate any requested condiments such as a pat of butter, a paper napkin and a knife and fork, even for a muffin. Never put food on top of a napkin. For carry-out orders, have packing procedures fixed – two paper napkins to the side, bag neatly rolled.

For new customers, point out where the napkins, cream and sugar are located. Follow up. Ask how they liked their beverage or food item. Ask if there's anything else they'd like. Stay open to feedback from customers, and keep them informed of changes and specials. Make sure they feel you think they are special, especially the familiar faces who are your loyal supporters.

If you learn this is someone's first visit, find out what brought the person into your coffeehouse – signs, ads, friends, the ambiance? When they leave, tell them you appreciate having them stop by and look forward to their next visit.

Train Them to Cope With Incidents
Life isn't perfect – mistakes happen and complaints will occur, often from an angry, frustrated customer. Listening to unhappy people can be painful, but your employees can be trained to handle a confrontation with grace. The first step is to recast customer upset as a concern, and your chance to improve service. Have employees

stop and give their full attention to the person speaking and to listen to the entire complaint.

At a staff meeting, have your employees practice appropriate responses, just as they would rehearse lines for a performance. You can play the unhappy customer and challenge them to respond calmly and learn from each other what works. It doesn't matter whose fault it is, the employee will apologize for the whole staff. "I'm so sorry it's not hot enough. We want you to be 100 percent happy here. Let me make you a fresh cup."

Train them to agree with the customer that the situation is unfortunate and requires a solution at once. "You're right. I'm so sorry. That's not what you asked for. I'll take care of that right now." Help your staff recognize that a complaint is actually pointing out a problem that may truly need attention, something that can be done better, a step toward higher levels of satisfaction and greater success.

Sometimes you know the customer is wrong. Someone may have caused them grief and you get the blame. That doesn't matter. A mistake happened, you admit it willingly, take full personal responsibility and offer something of value to pay for it, or you lose your credibility. To maintain client loyalty, compensation is required.

The best way to avoid errors and complaints is to make sure your people are well trained so they do things right. Make sure they know exactly what their responsibilities are. Put procedures in place and make sure employees follow them. And mistakes will happen, so be sure they are prepared to handle them.

> Help your staff recognize that a complaint is actually pointing out a problem ...

Dress Code and Other Policies

You want your representatives looking as good as your classy décor. A uniform shows professionalism and allows you more control over staff appearance. At the very least, have great looking aprons to be worn over a white shirt with dark pants. Require the kind of flawless personal grooming and careful dressing that can inspire respect and confidence in the food and beverages and in any information offered or sales suggestions made. Document your dress code and other policies. Post them and give everyone a copy.

In Italy, baristas study at trade schools and they stay with their jobs for years, often for a lifetime.

Work hours are rigidly fixed, breaks set in advance with no deviation. The prep person does not deal with barista activities. The bus person makes a pick-up round for newspapers and sweeping at a time interval you set. Who will empty the dishwasher? Who cleans up liquid spills and with what? Have a place where the mop goes and a rule that it's rinsed out here after each use. Make available some laminated opening and closing task lists so there are no questions about which shift does what.

Teach Technical Perfection

In Italy, even children display knowledge and passion about good coffee, but few Americans appreciate the nuances and the many variables that determine the final outcome. In Italy, baristas study at trade schools and they stay with their jobs for years, often for a lifetime. They have attitude and they get respect. Espresso is not a simple product. It's hardly rocket science but, as with gourmet cooking, excellence lives in the details.

Along Italy's Cinque Terra coast I met Mario, a former accountant. He said, "I love making coffee and working by the sea. We have many tourists and I find Americans think making espresso is simple. It is not. A change of weather has me constantly correcting the grind, to assure a good drink for my customers. I have traveled to many places, and nowhere can I find people who take coffee as seriously as we do in Italy."

In most of Europe, centuries of proud tradition infuse the professionals who serve quality food and drink. In America, people often see serving as a short-term job until they can find one that utilizes their potential. We can help overcome this kind of thinking by instilling real pride in this art form. Even the idea of an artistic pour can be taught when you understand the importance of the milk, steaming, pouring hearts and rosettes on top of the drinks. Train your baristas to do it right, knowing they will not always achieve perfection. Encourage your people to dump a cup that is not up to par. Your reputation depends on consistent quality.

A barista is a performer with a captive audience. This is doubly true in a small operation, where a charming and informative patter is part of the act. This is when the employee teaches, emphasizes the excellence of what is being prepared and builds a memorable experience. "Look at this crema, the golden layer of foam. This is where most of the flavor is found. It's what espresso is all about, extracting the aroma and taste of the essential oils."

To another person, the barista might say, "Our espresso is a blend of four beans, Brazilian Santos, Sumatran from a small estate in the northern part of the island, shade-grown Guatemalan from the highlands around Lake Atitlan, and Kenya AA grown on the slopes of Mt. Kenya."

This kind of information is marketing at its best, not slick come-ons but education that builds knowledge. People want to know why one coffee is better or different. If you sell your employees first, encouraging them to try everything and talk about it, they can share enthusiasm with the customer. The ability to articulate fine differences is the only way you have of creating value and credibility.

Teach employees to promote expertise and quality and to provide fascinating trivia. "Did you know the Pope blessed coffee and declared it a truly Christian beverage?" Or, "Do you know about the estate grown coffees we order from Nicaragua? Our owner visits to make sure this operation and others provide workers with proper housing and wages." If another customer appears, it's time to break off a moment to greet and let them know the wait won't be long. One who truly knows and loves coffee can talk about it with the same sort of affection wine-lovers display.

Train for Up-Selling

When an employee is skilled at making customers feel welcome, and at the details of doing her job, it's time to work on "up-selling," the gentle art of adding to the tab. Your example is their best inspiration. Though you understand it as a fundamental part of the job, few employees will consistently suggest another item without training and encouragement. In this business, volume is everything. If you can sell one additional item to every third person, you raise your yearly income by many thousands.

Don't try to oversell. The right offer to the right person is key. For the businessman who always orders a 12-ounce, why not suggest, "Our 16-ounce size is a great deal today." To the high school student, in the afternoon when teens often feel starved, "How about one of our strawberry lemon bars, fresh out of the oven?" For the senior who complained yesterday about his acid stomach, you can point out, "We have a wide selection of caffeine-free options for you — herbal teas, granita, our special white hot cocoa." You can also educate, pointing out that certain origin coffees produce less acidity.

An employee trained in suggestive selling and up-selling can dramatically increase your bottom line.

Train your people to assess what might really please a customer. Suggest juice for a child, a pound of your best beans for a man who says the coffee at the office is awful. People appreciate great suggestions such as an iced drink in warm weather, a tasty muffin in mid-morning, and at midday the salad on special this week.

An employee trained in suggestive selling and up-selling can dramatically increase your bottom line. If your average customer normally spends between one and two dollars on a cup of coffee, but you are able to sell some of them a pound of beans and a scone, you will have an additional $12 to $15 in your cash register. Multiply this number by dozens of transactions a day, and suggestions for what else to buy can turn an operation that is barely getting by or losing money into one that is making a handsome profit. One successful chain provided bonuses based on an individual's pastry, food and bean sales. It's easy to track these things with today's sophisticated systems.

If you expect your employees to sell home brewing equipment, they need to understand and love it. Have extras available so they can take them home and play with them. If they really like a product, they will sell it for you. Encourage customers to bring in machines and items they find confusing and show them how they work, then sell them the greatest coffee or tea to use at home. You become their hero, while the business that sold them the item fades into the background.

Teach Them to Teach

People love to learn about coffee. When someone on an airplane asks me what I do for a living, I usually don't go into detail. Time and time again I have found that once people know I'm in the coffee business, they ask me hundreds of questions about growing, roasting and proper brewing techniques. Often they say they don't drink coffee, but they still want to know more about the product. Often these three-hour in-flight teaching seminars leave me exhausted. But the point is, people love to learn about coffee.

In a small operation you have a one- to two-minute window of time to relate to your customers and sell them through teaching. All baristas in my operations knew about most aspects of the bean and I encouraged them to educate our customers when time permitted. I trained each employee to use this time to tell customers just how great our coffee was. I told my employees to engage customers, if we weren't too busy, suggesting to them that they watch an espresso extraction. This is when the barista can explain nuances of how their drink is prepared.

It's a chance too, to talk about the beans. In my operations, I purchased my coffee but did not roast. After tasting coffee from a dozen roasters, in my opinion, the coffee beans I chose for my operations were the finest in the world. My Seattle roaster had a penchant for quality, and either my employees or I would tell new customers that we could buy coffee for half of what we paid, but that the flavor profile and complexity of ours was unmatched. We then encouraged them to try it and compare it to coffee from other coffeehouses.

Planting that seed helped customers to fine-tune their palates and to notice what they were drinking. We hoped that our educational effort would pay off, and that the next time they bought coffee at another establishment they would realize the coffee did not have the same nuances and complexity as the coffee they purchased at our business.

Wine is the only other beverage that sparks as much interest as coffee. People are fascinated by wine lists and love to share with others their opinion of a certain varietal, region or year. Coffee is now garnering the same interest. Train your people to use the up-swell of interest in coffee to your advantage as you market your product.

CHAPTER 8

SELLING THE BEANS

An extremely important decision you will need to make as a coffee retailer is "how" or "if" you should market whole-bean coffee in your operation. Most retailers choose to sell beans for their customers to consume at home for the obvious reason that these sales drive home their brand and bring customers back to replenish their supply. We believe it is an excellent idea to make whole-bean sales a part of your overall sales mix.

First and foremost, you are in the coffee business. That's why marketing your fine coffee beans is an important part of marketing your entire business. You want to convince your customers that you serve the best beans available anywhere. If you're not already selling coffee by the pound, would whole-bean sales work for you?

Of the 300 million cups of coffee Americans drink each day, about three-quarters are brewed at home.

Many specialty coffee businesses behave as if they have no control over what customers purchase, that they are operating at the whim of the marketplace and if people come in for a cup of coffee or other bar drink, they are not likely to buy beans. They see that those who sell whole beans successfully have built up their reputation over a number of years. Yet, we have found that anyone can promote whole-bean coffee and make it profitable.

Of the 300 million cups of coffee Americans drink each day, about three-quarters are brewed at home. Though the retail beverage business is a great model for success, these numbers suggest that you miss a large potential market if you don't also sell beans for your customers to brew at home.

Certainly, many people will continue to buy inexpensive canned coffee or grind their own at the better grocery stores. But for customers with great brewing equipment, whole beans are an obvious purchase when they drop by your store to take a break. Bean sales can bring substantial profits to any coffee retail operation.

Consider also selling home brewing accessories of every sort. Customers who come in for an espresso may see your retail display and ask questions. Starting a conversation about the comparative merits of gold filters, press pots and pour-over cones nearly always leads to the sale of a device or of beans.

The premium bean display must be clearly visible, attractive and easy to approach. But a good bean display is only as good as the staff you train to clearly explain the value of origin coffees and the unique taste and story behind them. So, what should you promote?

Three categories of beans sell consistently to the right customers. Organically grown coffees appeal to those with environmental concerns. Estate coffees can be attractive because of their very high quality or because of the excellent social and labor practices that producers espouse. Flavorful decaffeinated beans appeal to those with health concerns and can be sold to gourmets as the ideal after-dinner coffee.

The next question is, Whose beans will you sell?
Your three options include:
1. Roasting your own on a small or large scale.
2. Buying someone else's beans to market under your own private label.
3. Buying a well-known brand and promoting it as the best in the area.

Let's look at each of these scenarios and compare the differences and similarities in marketing each of them.

Roasting Your Own

For a number of reasons, a majority of coffee operations don't roast their own beans. Most discover that it's too expensive to purchase and operate a full-size roaster if they plan to roast for only one or two retail stores. You could purchase a small batch roaster and roast only a few pounds of beans at a time, but roasting in this manner is very time consuming and often leads to an inconsistent product.

Sometimes small retailers open what is called a "roasteria," where the coffee roaster is in prominent view. It can be in the front window of the store or behind a glass wall so customers can watch the roasting process. Why the glass wall? Roasting coffee does not smell as great as you might think and the smell is powerful. If you decide to set up a roasteria, you'll need to install major exhaust equipment to deal with the odor and the gases emitted by the roasting process. And be sure zoning allows you to roast in that neighborhood.

I know a number of successful coffeehouses that roast in-store. However, I recommend you don't start roasting until after the rest of your operation is running smoothly. And that could take months, or even years. Roasting is an art form. You'll need a very different set of skills than the ones you use to manage and market the retail part of your operation. During planning, design and build-out, some retailers set aside an area for a future roaster and then develop the space when the business is ready to expand into roasting.

One advantage of roasting your own coffee is that your employees will learn more about the coffee bean.

If you decide to roast your own coffee, I advise you to hire an experienced roaster and put him or her in charge of this part of your operation. If this is not possible, spend your money wisely and hire a roasting consultant to help you learn the process. Once your roasted coffee is at the point of excellence, you're ready to secure accounts and sell your coffee wholesale. Wholesaling will promote your name and your retail business, especially if you can convince some high-profile restaurants in your area to serve your excellent coffee.

When you roast your own, staff will have to be trained to take on the important responsibility of promoting your custom roasting service. Brewed samples allow customers to compare the mild, medium and dark roasts and see which they prefer. As you hand out a sample, talk about how to brew a perfect cup and quantities to use for mild, medium or strong taste. Give out your brochure explaining your sources and roasting. Education can be the key to success.

One advantage of roasting your own coffee is that your employees will learn more about the coffee bean. If you expose employees to roasting, they will soon learn about origin coffees and the differences in taste between them. As a result, they should soon be knowledgeable enough to discuss your various coffees more intelligently with your customers.

Another advantage of roasting is that your customers assume you are more involved with all aspects of coffee and far better informed than retailers who don't roast. Customers will see that you are serious about serving the freshest coffee possible. Smart roasters will make freshness a focus of their marketing campaign. Even though roasting is a huge undertaking, it can generate enormous marketing power.

Private Label Coffee

Many coffee operations buy beans in bulk from a specific roaster and then re-bag or sticker them with their own name and logo. This process is known as private labeling. Operations that private label may never let the consumer know that the beans they sell are roasted by another company. However, if your customers ask, you should be honest. Tell them you didn't roast the beans, but that they were roasted to your strict specifications by a reputable roaster.

Market both your own roasted coffee and coffee that you sell under a private label in similar ways. Develop a specific name for each blend, a name that captures the spirit of your business. For example, you might consider calling a highly caffeinated blend "Raging Tiger" or a decaffeinated blend "Quiet Brook." You can do the same with your tea blends, which we will discuss in a future chapter.

> Find a roasting company that knows coffee and is passionate about what it does.

If you have decided to create your own private label, first interview numerous companies and choose the very best supplier you can find. Roasters and the coffee they produce vary, like any other company's product.

Find a roasting company that:
- Knows coffee and is passionate about what it does
- Understands the art of blending (imperative for your espresso coffee)
- Understands your need to promote your brand
- Provides excellent customer service and exhibits professionalism
- Has an excellent packaging program and offers help with bag design and labels

Once you've chosen your supplier, packaging is your next step in marketing. Ka-Pak bags work well. Custom, stick-on labels for each coffee variety can be colorful and unique. Allow space to write in the roast date. A place for the roast master's name personalizes your operation and gives the customer someone to call if the coffee is not quite perfect.

Selling Their Beans

Many retailers decide to sell another roaster's beans instead of creating a private label. If yours is a new operation, you'll have good reasons to do just that. For example, if you sell and promote XYZ's coffee, the company will often supply you with marketing materials and signage to help you sell their coffee. They are invested in your success.

One big advantage in selling someone else's coffee is name recognition.

One Portland supplier gives their retailers a new full-color poster each month to help them with promotional efforts. The owner of a single operation or small chain will have a difficult time offering any better marketing punch. When looking for the right roaster, when you decide to sell and promote another roaster's coffee, inquire about what marketing programs and equipment they may offer.

Many large roasting companies open their own retail operations to promote their brands, but they are roasters first and retailers second. They often will not put serious effort into retailing, the way you can. Your retail business can be far more effective selling roasted beans than many of the roasters themselves. Two roasters in Los Angeles told me they were losing money on their retail operations, but that they continued to keep them open to promote brand awareness. Roasters are not your competition.

One big advantage in selling someone else's coffee is name recognition. If the supplier has a good reputation in a given demographic area, and a large following, you won't have to convince your customers how great their beans are. When a customer buys beans, let them know what variety will be on special the following week and encourage them to try other coffees.

Your Bean Display

Most small retail coffee operations have a few things to learn about marketing and displaying the coffee they sell by the pound. The chains do it very well. Visit other cafés and see what they do. The successful ones not only have signage with the names of their origin coffees, but they also have a display of pre-packaged coffee near the cash register to spur the impulse buy.

If possible, use images from the origin country on your signage. If you insist on small bins, keep them clean. Don't allow oil to build up on any glass or plastic surface.

Educate Every Employee About Every Coffee

As we discussed under the heading of employees, you must educate your staff about your coffees so they can explain them to your customers. Make sure they watch "The Passionate Harvest," the award-winning and definitive film that chronicles coffee production from seed to cup. The film was written by world-renowned coffee expert Ken Davids and directed by me. This exceptional training tool is distributed by Bellissimo. In one hour, this film will transport viewers around the world and further a deep appreciation for the product.

When you sell beans, your employees need to understand more about coffee so they can educate customers. As part of ongoing training, encourage each employee to read books on how coffee is grown so they know the stories behind such varieties as Kenya AA and Sumatra. Teach them to recommend coffees to customers based on the customer's palate. The credibility of your operation is at risk when a customer asks detailed questions about your coffee beans and you or your employees can't provide convincing answers.

> When you sell beans, your employees need to understand more about coffee so they can educate customers.

When a customer is interested in buying whole beans, your employees should ask what method will be used to prepare coffee at home. Discourage customers from having their coffee ground unless they intend to use it quickly. If the customer insists on having you grind the coffee, use the grinder setting compatible with the brewing method to be used. And see this as an opportunity to sell a coffee grinder.

Up-selling the Beans

You can double or triple your whole-bean sales if you train your employees to up-sell your customers. Teach your staff to recommend whole-bean coffees to your beverage customers and to stress a special or a coffee of the month. For example, tell customers about a great coffee that just came in, one only available in limited quantities and at certain times of the year. Then recommend buying this extraordinary coffee before it sells out.

Keep it Simple

Customers can become confused and discouraged by too many choices. Some operators make the mistake of carrying too many types of coffee. Other operators carry only an espresso blend and two or three of their house coffee blends. For true coffee connoisseurs in a sophisticated urban location, this will not be enough. But if you don't sell a lot of whole-bean coffee, it's wise to limit the number of coffees you sell.

In addition, if you overstock and undersell whole beans, much of your product may go stale before it sells. Because coffee has a limited shelf life, begin your bean marketing campaign slowly. Find out what coffees your customers like and try not to roast or buy them too far in advance. Never sell stale beans. You want to be known as the place that offers the best and the freshest coffee beans in your area.

With proper marketing, you can generate additional income by selling whole-bean coffee. Only you know which marketing method will work for your area, the size of your operation and your clientele. No matter which tack you take, approach it with passion, knowledge and flair.

To help you begin selling beans, here's a list of some of the origin coffees Bellissimo suggests to its clients:
- Guatemalan Antigua
- Kona Estate
- Ethiopian Yergacheffe
- Brazilian Santos
- Kenya AA
- Sumatra Mandheling
- Costa Rican Tarrazu

CHAPTER 9

MARKET SMALL WARES AND RETAIL ITEMS

Everyone who comes into your coffee bar for a beverage is a potential customer for brewing equipment and other attractive retail items, small and large. If you have display space, you can win those extra sales by offering a great selection of items to pull extra dollars to your bottom line each month.

Choose merchandise to sell that complements the theme of your store. Then display it where your staff can see all of it easily, to avoid shrinkage (theft). Since you probably won't need extra employees to staff the retail area, the only cost associated with running this additional profit center is the display area set-up and the wholesale price of the gift items. Because of the 50 percent margin on most of items, many coffee shops are able to generate an additional $35,000 to $40,000 in profit each fiscal year. It takes minimal time to order items and stock the area, and many owners actually feel the displays add a favorable dimension to their business.

It's not all fun. Selling coffee accessories can be a challenge, with so many competing retailers offering similar items. Therefore, look for the unique! A coffee bar will not have the buying power to offer mugs, grinders and brewing equipment at discount prices. Department stores, mass merchandisers and specialty grocery and kitchen shops all want that business. But, if you've trained your employees correctly, your customers have learned from your people about beans and fine brewing and trust you in matters of coffee. They naturally expect you to carry good tools for at-home brewing of the superb beans you sell.

If your coffeehouse has a unique theme or is located in a tourist area, you might want to sell various theme gift items. For example, I once consulted for the owner of a 2000 square foot coffee bar located in a town in the hills of New Mexico. The town drew thousands of tourists each year, and as a result, the coffee bar was able to sell an unbelievable quantity of theme-based gifts from a 12'x12' fenced-in area. One of the most popular items was a string of chili pepper lights that captured the spirit of the area's food and culture. From this small space, the business generated more than $65,000 a year in net sales.

Create Another Reason to Visit

By offering retail items, you create an additional customer draw, a reason to patronize your business rather than the competition. A number of people will visit your coffee bar regularly, attracted by the delightful atmosphere and warm friendly service. They like your choice of music. They like your employees and they love your coffee. Why not give them one more reason to come in?

In my Portland neighborhood, a small coffee bar has a long wall, stocked from floor to ceiling with retail merchandise. Most items are coffee-related, but some are small gift items. The buyer does a great job sourcing unusual items, and often when I need to pick up a small birthday or wedding gift, I think of this coffee bar as a convenient place to shop.

Some mornings as I sit and read the paper and drink a cup of coffee at this coffee bar, I see customers peruse the retail merchandise and purchase a $20 to $30 item. These may very well be impulse buys. Your customers may not plan to purchase a shower or birthday gift at a coffee bar, but if you offer retail merchandise, they might see an item that fits the occasion and buy it because it is convenient.

Gifts, at a coffee bar? Today, time is a precious commodity. People look for convenience in their day-to-day lives. If you can offer items in your store that they would need to make a special trip to buy elsewhere, they may purchase from you just to save time. Sell items that people want for themselves as well as those that make suitable gifts for friends and relatives. Small, inexpensive items like coffee candies, coffee-theme greeting cards and such will sell quickly and on impulse.

Where to Find Retail Items
Gift shows are a great place to look for gift and theme items. Ask other shop owners which shows are the best in your region. Though attending a show can be a big effort, there's no better way to keep up on trends and to see what designers and manufacturers offer that's new, attractive and cutting edge.

Almost every city of a million or more has annual gift trade shows where you can buy small items to sell at your business. Many major cities also have large Gift Marts (Seattle, Dallas, San Francisco, and Los Angeles, in the West) filled with showrooms staffed by helpful product representatives that are open year round to those who possess a business card.

You will also find many items to sell at food industry trade shows. The Fancy Food Show (see Chapter 2) is held three times a year in San Francisco, Chicago and New York, and is the best place to find unusual food-related items like jams, biscotti, candies or chocolates.

Some catalog businesses specialize in small wares for you and your baristas to use on the job. But if you study those catalogs closely, you'll find that the companies also sell many items that are appropriate for your customers. Two such companies are Espresso Supply (www.espressosupply.com) and Visions Espresso (www.visionsespresso.com), both of Seattle.

...to keep up on trends in your industry, you can use these shows to locate the newest retail items.

You will, of course, find great retail merchandise at coffee industry trade shows. When I first started attending these shows years ago, most exhibitor booths were dedicated to espresso machines and coffee. Today, you will find booths devoted to coffee jewelry, mugs, chocolates, and teas — items you can sell in the retail section of your operation. Since you'd be wise to attend a few shows each year to keep up on trends in your industry, you can use these shows to locate the newest retail items.

As we noted in Chapter 2, the largest industry trade show is the annual Specialty Coffee Association of America Conference & Exhibition usually held in April. Coffee Fest trade shows generally occur three times each year, in spring, summer and fall. NASCORE, sponsored by *Fresh Cup Magazine,* takes place in either September or October. These shows are in different cities each year, so visit their Web sites for up-to-date schedules. Each show will have numerous booths devoted to items for your retail shelves. (See Chapter 2 for information on how to contact these trade shows.)

What to Sell

Use your imagination and knowledge of your customer base to help you decide what to sell. If your operation is on the coast of Maine you probably won't want to display the hanging chili pepper lights that sold like hot cakes in New Mexico.

If you've spent a great deal of effort convincing people that your beans and beverages are the best in the area, keep pace with that level of quality in the selection of retail items you offer. The quality of your merchandise will reflect on your entire business. Choose items that fit in with your existing product lines and reflect both your business plan and the theme of your store.

Make your store the ultimate resource for home brewing of the finest coffees and teas. By stocking the full range of related items you make your store first choice with serious consumers, giving you a competitive edge. A unique selection of superior accessories, kept clean and beautifully displayed, can certainly increase your bottom line.

Every new area of business is risky, so do some research. Look at the other retailers around you. If there's a gourmet kitchen shop across the street, don't offer the same brands of espresso maker that they sell. Look at the social and cultural demographics of your area and your customer. Upper-income women in a neighborhood of boutiques and galleries are more likely to buy a home espresso machine than are men on break from the paint wholesaler next door. Practice due diligence before you purchase, but don't be afraid to try something a bit edgy. Once you have some sales history on retail items, you'll know what works for you and your customers.

The old "80-20 rule" applies to every retail operation. Eighty percent of your sales come from 20 percent of your inventory selection. Be sure your cash register is set up to keep records so you know which items are included in the 20 percent. Make it your goal to constantly improve and expand the variety and quality of products in that category, and to see if new items will be as popular.

> The old "80-20 rule" applies to every retail operation. Eighty percent of your sales come from 20 percent of your inventory selection.

High on the list of top-selling gift items are small bottles of flavored syrups, travel mugs and gift baskets. Let your knowledge of your area, what the competition carries and your store theme point you to retail items that will set you apart. The items listed below normally sell well no matter where your business is located.

- Coffee Devices and Products:
  - home grinders
  - thermal holding pots
  - to-go or travel mugs with your logo
  - French press brewers (2 sizes)
  - airtight whole-bean containers
  - home espresso machines
  - ceramic mugs of all sizes and shapes
  - demitasse cups
  - thermometers, brewing guides, steaming pitchers

- Coffee-flavored candies and chocolates

- T-shirts and sweatshirts with your logo or a coffee theme

- Tea-related items:
  - teapots
  - gift boxes with special teas
  - tea bag plates
  - brewing devices

- Unique coffee scoops

- Books on coffee and tea

- Coffee- or tea-themed jewelry

- Specialty chocolates

- Music CDs with an ethnic theme

- Small gift items that mirror your theme

- Flavoring syrups (large and small sizes)

- Seasonal gift baskets that include coffee

The two most generally popular items at coffee and teashops are mugs and teapots. Other popular items include drip coffee makers, thermal carafes, stovetop espresso makers, permanent and paper filters, electric and stovetop teakettles and tea-related items like infusers.

Among the most popular items in winter holiday gift baskets are coffees, teas and hot chocolate mixes. By late fall, you can stock baskets containing these items, and tempt some of those $3 cappuccino customers to make a $35 purchase while doing their planned holiday shopping effortlessly.

Let your own theme guide you to other appropriate ideas. If your coffee business has an Italian theme, you might want to carry some small gift items from Italy, such as murano glass and colorful hand-painted ceramics. Food items like beautifully bottled olive oil can sell well, too.

How and How Much to Display

In setting up a new retail display in an established shop, don't make the mistake of crowding out your loyal regulars. Reduced seating, especially at busy hours, will add stress. You want your customers to feel comfortable despite changes. And you certainly don't want the display to slow down your beverage service. Avoid piling up new merchandise and rows of mugs on existing surfaces, where they may get in the way and be a distraction.

Attractive, well-placed signs are critical to successfully merchandising all parts of your business. Signs get attention. They should be bright, colorful, with large lettering, and fonts that are both easy to read and artistically attractive. Allocate money in your merchandising budget for quality signs that will motivate a response to your merchandise.

Well-lighted wall shelves, easily visible from the service counter, work well for brewing equipment in many shops. Attractive, more expensive items that are easy to see from seating areas will get the attention of people enjoying a moment of leisure. Staff members can appear to answer questions when a customer looks interested. Some shops find that islands where people stand in line are more likely to elicit the quick impulse purchase, especially of low-priced items like mugs.

Keep it simple, especially at first. Don't make the mistake of displaying too many unrelated items in too many different places.

From a marketing perspective, if you are opening a coffee bar, don't make your retail area the main focus of your store. If you do, your customers will think you are in the business of selling gifts, not coffee. You never want your customers to be puzzled about what you do.

Effective displays create the welcoming and exciting mood that is a large part of effective merchandising.

One retailer I worked with in Massachusetts was confused about the importance of emphasizing that he was operating a coffee shop. Against my advice, he devoted almost half of his store to ceramic items. Every person I spoke with in this beautiful coffee bar would ask, "Is this a coffee bar or a store?" The large retail area definitely distracted the customers from the real focus of the business – great coffee. And to add insult to injury, the retail merchandise sold poorly. The retailer lost his coffee identity while confusing his customers. Had he used less space to display his retail items and devoted the area to seating and a stage for evening entertainment, I am sure he would have been more successful.

Think of your retail display as part of the merchandising that begins with the first impression made, the moment someone walks into your store. A beautiful display of colorful and striking retail items, under sparkling halogen lights, is a great addition to the decor.

Effective displays create the welcoming and exciting mood that is a large part of effective merchandising, defined as the promotion of products that occurs inside your business. Along with the overall ambiance of your shop, great product displays help generate more customer traffic, amplify repeat business, increase numbers of people who buy items and how much they actually spend.

Markup

To arrive at the retail price of retail merchandise, you should at least double the wholesale price and add shipping. This practice is known as "keystoning." Most retailers keystone their merchandise.

For example, if you purchase a dozen mugs at $5 each and the company you purchase them from charges you $10 for shipping, you have invested a total of $70, or $5.83, in each mug. If there are no other costs associated with the mugs (for example a charge for printing your logo and name on them), most shops would sell them at retail for $11.95 each.

You won't want to keystone all the items you sell. Look at the big picture. For example, if you sell a French press with a pound of coffee, it might be a good idea to give your customer a great deal on the brewing device. If your customer buys the French press, she may continue to buy beans from you for the life of the appliance and you will make significantly more in the long run. This especially makes sense if you roast your own coffee, and have well over a 100 percent markup on your beans.

To stay competitive in pricing strategy, you need to be aware of what other retailers offer nearby. With more competition, customer response to price becomes more sensitive. If you can provide good reasons for higher prices, you may still make the sale.

Train staff members on every aspect of a new product. Friendly personal attention and thorough knowledge of all your merchandise will win customers and sometimes allow you to charge more than the big box stores.

Special Promotions
A good way to promote add-on sales is by informing people about how to use your products. This can be accomplished by conducting some free informational classes. You might start with an evening event on home espresso preparation and another on selecting, storing and preparing the finest coffees. Interactive classes, where people try things in small groups and get to know each other, are much more fun than the lecture-demo format. To promote these events use flyers or handouts in addition to signs in the store.

> A good way to promote add-on sales is by informing people about how to use your products.

You do not have to sell retail merchandise to be successful in this business, but a well thought-out and unique selection of items can increase your net sales and ultimately, your bottom line. Visit your competitors and coffee bars in other cities. See what items other coffee operators are selling and how they market them. Check out specialty catalogs and trade shows, as well as Web sites. Then decide which items will sell best for you, and market them enthusiastically.

CHAPTER 10

POLITICALLY CONSCIOUS, EARTH-FRIENDLY PRODUCTS

The Specialty Coffee Association of America (SCAA) says the growth rate of organic coffee sales is twice that of specialty coffees in general, and increasing every year. But before you offer organic coffee, assess your market. What do your own customers value and what makes your coffee bar stand out from others in the area?

Consumers are becoming more conscious of the origins of products and making purchases based on their personal ethics, the specialty coffee customer even more so. They know what the term organic implies, and they likely understand the concept of estate coffees.

Many specialty coffee drinkers are highly educated, concerned about poisonous pesticides and herbicides, and personally health conscious.

Many coffee bar customers believe organic products are inherently better and also value an environmentally friendly product. Many specialty coffee drinkers are highly educated, concerned about poisonous pesticides and herbicides, and personally health conscious. They prefer products that reflect high ethical standards to protect the land as well as native bird and animal life, and workers' rights and health.

Large companies have certainly seen this trend and in my opinion have often exploited these causes for financial gain. If their marketing results help the world, then little harm is done. However, in today's cynical world, it's much easier for the independent coffee operation or small chain to show more sincerity when it comes to "cause" marketing. For one thing, your customers know that estate and organic coffees are produced only in small quantities and understand that often the large chains can't manage to fully utilize this premium resource.

Some History

Traditional non-specialty coffee marketing is well established in a mature market. Three huge corporations provide about three-quarters of the coffee sold in the U.S. Phillip Morris/Kraft, Proctor & Gamble and Nestlé spend over $300 million annually to advertise coffee. In the past 50 years, coffee quality has dropped and consumption is down dramatically. In the 50s, 75 percent of adults drank three to four cups per day. Today half of adults drink coffee and they average fewer than two cups per day.

The only force tending to reverse this trend is the appeal of specialty coffees. Between 1970 and 2000, specialty coffee grew in popularity at the same time as the big multinational firms lost one third of their coffee sales. The specialty coffee business is now valued at almost nine billion dollars per year in the U. S. But specialty coffee too is becoming more like a commodity as it grows more standardized and competitive.

People want choices and they want a superior product. Dark-roasted beans and the espresso machines at every gas station quick-stop no longer meet America's wish for something unique and better.

Customers with a conscience can be passionate about farm-identified and socially responsible coffee, and coffee produced using organic and sustainable agricultural practices. You can tap into the passions of those customers with a long-term commitment to the people who supply your specialty beans, and by being creative in using issues marketing to promote and sell a unique product.

Wise Marketing

If you have ever visited a coffee-producing country, you likely returned with a deep and sincere appreciation for coffee and the people who make your morning cup possible. Viewing our video, "The Passionate Harvest," will give any employee or owner of a coffee business a deep understanding of the hard work and sacrifice involved in getting those small brown beans to market. Many coffee operations play the video without sound, to open up a dialogue between customers and employees about how coffee travels from seed to cup.

If you have ever visited a coffee-producing country, you likely returned with a deep and sincere appreciation for coffee and the people who make your morning cup possible.

After traveling around the world from Guatemala to Africa to make that prize-winning video, it became very clear to Ken and me that coffee is a bargain. The workers who produce excellent coffee deserve fair wages, education and a livable planet. Unfortunately, this does not always happen. Many retailers are creating an awareness of the plight of these workers by marketing fair-trade and eco-friendly coffees that benefit the workers and their environment.

With more consumers caring more about the political and environmental implications of what they drink, the specialty coffee business has become more competitive. The trend is toward coffees with both outstanding and unique character and political and environmental benefits.

The certification process legitimizes the claims of these coffees, providing evidence of a chain of careful custody from grower to retailer. "Farm-identified" and other certified coffees from socially responsible organic producers satisfy the new consumer demand, and offer you opportunities for sales.

Confusion in the Marketplace

Terms like eco-friendly, fair-trade, shade-grown and bird-friendly can be very confusing, even to those of us in the specialty coffee industry. Boost your coffee credibility by learning what each of these terms mean, and by selling at least some coffee with environmental and ethical certifications.

Educate yourself and your staff so you can responsibly answer questions from customers who inquire about these terms and ask for coffees with a particular seal of approval. Most likely you will not carry all the specific types, but you should do your homework and be able to respond with authority to customers who ask about any of them. Over the past few years these certifications have become important to more customers.

Here is a brief synopsis of some of the different types of socially responsible coffees:

- **Eco-Friendly Coffee:** This growing movement among coffee producers seeks to protect the environment, and more and more farmers are reducing or eliminating the use of chemicals, pesticides and artificial fertilizer in their production practices. Conventional coffee is one of the most chemically intensive crops. Before a grower can be certified organic, several years of production must pass during which all traces of artificial chemicals gradually fade away in the environment.
- **Organic Coffee:** Organic coffee is the fastest growing segment in specialty coffees, though it still only represents five percent of the specialty coffee sold. Organic coffee is grown without the use of synthetic chemicals — no chemical fertilizers, pesticides or herbicides. Coffee can be certified organic in one of three ways: direct certification, co-certification or local certification. In direct certification, a representative of an internationally accredited certifying organization must visit the farm, processor or exporter and certify the coffee. In co-certification, an

internationally certified organization supervises the work of a local organization. In local certification, an accreditation body certifies a local organization.

- **Fair-Trade Coffee:** For a coffee to be certified fair-trade in the United States, it must meet the standards established by TransFair USA (www.transfairusa.org). Certified fair-trade farmers are guaranteed a set minimum price above the cost of production so they receive a living wage in exchange for their beans, even if the coffee market is depressed. The goal of the fair-trade movement is to focus on the economics of the harvest to improve living conditions for coffee farmers everywhere.
- **Shade-Grown Coffee:** Coffee bushes thrive in partly shady habitats. Shade-grown coffee, about one percent of the specialty market, is grown under a canopy of shade trees that provide bio-diversity and habitat for birds and other species. This type of farming, in contrast to growing coffee on "clear-cut" hillsides with no large trees, is good for the soil and decreases the need for fertilizer. When landslides associated with Hurricane Mitch destroyed many farms in Nicaragua and Honduras, hillside coffee farms with large shade trees survived.

Third-party inspectors follow criteria established by the Smithsonian Migratory Bird Center (SMBC) or the Rainforest Alliance (the Eco OK label) to certify coffee as shade-grown. For more information visit www.rainforestalliance.org and http://natzoo.si.edu/ConservationAndScience/MigratoryBirds/Coffee/default.cfm

- **Bird-Friendly Coffee:** This coffee is shade-grown with a focus on an environment that protects the habitat of native and migratory birds and other wildlife. Because of the ongoing destruction over huge regions of the large canopy trees of the tropical highland rainforest, many bird species can only find shelter in the canopy of shaded coffee plantations. Bird Friendly™ coffees are certified using the same criteria as shade-grown coffee through the SMBC. For more information visit www.songbird.org
- **Relationship Coffee:** In relationship coffee, local producers deal directly with coffee roasters, cutting out the middleman in the coffee chain. This leads to higher prices for growers, who are encouraged to produce extraordinary coffees.

Farm-identified and estate coffees are two other well known specialty coffee categories, but their beans may or may not be grown using environmentally and socially responsible practices. They can complement the others, bringing their fame and excellence to your business.

I suggest you research socially responsible coffees and learn more about them. Then, following your passion and the mission statement of your business, choose which types of coffees and certifications are important to you. If you buy your beans, ask your roaster for more information about what coffees he carries with which certifications. If you are a micro-roaster, contact companies like Sustainable Harvest (www.sustainableharvest.com) or Equal Exchange (www.equalexchange.com) that specialize in selling green coffee with various certifications.

Learn from the Chains

A friend of mine in California owned a coffee bar across the street from a major U.S. chain store. The chain ran ads in the local newspaper and put large signs in their windows advertising that they served fair-trade certified coffee. My friend immediately designed a large banner on her computer and went to her local sign company and had two signs made announcing the same.

My friend knew she had to compete head-to-head with this chain or lose certain customers. Her operation was in a socially-conscious part of the city, so who do you think customers believed had the most passion about serving this type of coffee, the mega chain or the independent coffeehouse? One Saturday morning shortly after this battle began, I counted six people sitting in the chain store and over 60 in her coffeehouse!

Let Your Customers Know

One key to success in marketing certified coffees is to educate your employees about the issues surrounding them so that when customers ask about these coffees, your staff can provide good answers. It's not easy to explain the value of sustainable coffees. Posters, videos and story telling are essential. More specialty suppliers are supplying visual tools to help the retailer. Sophisticated point-of-sale signs and brochures bring the average coffee drinker into the rich and fascinating world of unique coffees.

With good promotional materials, feature one or two certified coffees in your advertising and marketing. You might want to hang a framed sign in your store describing the certification process, or print the information on the back of your punch cards. You can create a flyer explaining what certified coffees you serve and why you sell them. One of my clients designed a table tent with monthly specials on one side and, on the other, the story of their mission to help save the environment by selling eco-friendly coffee.

In addition, you can go one step further by making sure your cups and sleeves are eco-friendly. Some cups and other paper products are made of recycled paper and printed with earth-friendly ink.

Educate about Misleading Standards

There are many farms, regions and entire countries where coffee is grown using earth-friendly practices. However, many farmers in Guatemala can't afford to have their coffee inspected and certified as shade grown. Other farmers around the world grow their coffee trees in shade, and use no pesticides. They do it right and provide habit for local birds and animals, and yet their coffee has no certification of any kind. Why not? Because they can't afford inspections.

> You can create a flyer explaining what certified coffees you serve and why you sell them.

Highland farmers of Ethiopia grow some of the finest coffee in the world and over 90 percent of it would pass the rigors of any certification process. But most coffee in Ethiopia is grown in small backyard plots. The poor farmers take their small crop, nurtured to perfection, to a nearby depot. The brokers there represent a company that buys from farmers and finally delivers it to the capital in Addis Ababa. Although the coffee is most often eco-friendly in every way, it is not certified due to the expense of the certification process. You and your employees need to be aware of this. Great coffee from countries like Ethiopia and Guatemala should not be undervalued because the economy is undeveloped and the farmers can't afford certification.

Most of us in the coffee business, large and small, care deeply about workers' rights and the environment. Let's hope that in time we will see real progress made towards better lives for those who grow our specialty coffees. Support organizations like Coffee Kids (www.coffeekids.org) that work to improve the lives of coffee workers around the world.

We all need to work toward the day when more money ends up in the pockets of the growers and workers than in the coffers of the rich and powerful multinational corporations. So be wise, and do your small part by marketing these life-friendly products and becoming a responsible member of our planetary community.

CHAPTER 11

MARKETING OF OTHER BEVERAGES AND FOOD

If you walked into a coffee bar in the early days of specialty coffee, you could expect to be served an espresso-based beverage. If you wanted brewed coffee, you would more than likely be handed an Americano. There weren't a lot of choices. As the industry grew and developed, new products and beverage innovations began to appear at every industry trade show.

A number of years ago when drive-thrus were still a new phenomena, I was involved with a group of people that came up with a new twist on the concept – a drive-thru that focused on coffee, but that also offered a wide range of other beverages. At that time, every drive-thru we visited served coffee products – period. We brainstormed and discussed the idea of offering soft-serve ice cream, which we could use in the smoothies we wanted to include on the menu. We thought also about offering juices and panini. Well, the industry has caught up with our ideas and then some!

Quality is one area where you can compete with even the largest operations.

Competition can push you to consider expanding your food and drink menu. If your neighborhood has several other shops like yours, or if you learn that a national chain will open nearby, you need a way to make your operation unique. A wider selection of products can create the advantage you may need to survive and thrive. As other coffee bars expand their menus, you may have little choice but to use menu expansion to compete.

Certainly you'll have to make an investment to expand your offerings, but if you can predict that selling panini sandwiches, deli salads, granita, rare teas, smoothies, fruit juices and more will solve some economic problems, don't hesitate to buy that extra equipment. Few operations can generate high levels of sales on coffee alone.

Before you invest, assess your target market. Teens near a high school will want different options than you'd offer in a hospital setting, or a financial district. Regional and ethnic preferences, climate and socio-economic level will all influence what you can sell. Don't try to be a quick-stop market. You are first and always a quality coffee operation, so choose only the finest products. Quality is the one area where you can compete with even the largest operations.

Fine Wine and Special Beer

After visiting hundreds of coffee bars in Italy over the years, I began to think that in the right location, offering beer and wine was a good idea to attract evening customers in the U.S. Today, more and more of Bellissimo's clients are adding these beverages to their menus to attract customers during times of day when they aren't selling much coffee. Remember it's highly unlikely the mega coffee chains will ever offer alcohol, so take advantage of this fact and set your operation apart from them in yet another way.

I worked with a retailer in the South who designed a beautiful coffee bar with an Italian theme. His coffee bar was so gorgeous and authentic, that if you didn't know better, you could almost believe you were in Rome or Milan. His location seemed mediocre at best, but it was near a performing arts center that provided his business with ample evening traffic. He sold wine by the bottle and the glass, and at any given time he offered a selection of six to eight different varietals. He also stocked some very unusual beers and sold them for premium prices. To go with this menu of beer and wine, he offered light food items that were easy to prepare, such as panini, cheese plates and capresi salads. The last time I checked in with him, he told me his evening menu was outperforming his morning and afternoon coffee sales by a ratio of two to one.

At Bellissimo, we field calls every day from people who are interested in the viability of selling beer and wine. I tell them that offering these options is a growing trend, and that the liquor and coffee industries have started to take notice of each other. At a spirits show I attended in Las Vegas, a number of coffee companies were exhibitors. The wine industry in particular has expressed strong interest in penetrating the coffee market.

If done properly, you can keep your identity as a coffee business and still offer beer and wine.

If done properly, you can keep your identity as a coffee business and still offer beer and wine. It's all about giving your customers the menu options they want and creating the proper ambiance.

Tea: The Next Big Thing
Tea has been a world favorite for thousands of years, and is popular everywhere. The beverage is known as Chai in India, Russia, the

Middle East and Central Asia. It's Tsae in Greek, Cha in China and Korea, Te in Fijian and Spanish and The' in French.

The tea plant is a bush called Camellia sinensis or Thea sinensis, producing tender young leaves with some caffeine. Tea is grown not only in the traditional highland locations in Asia but also in mountainous areas of Africa, Turkey and South America. See more at www.planet-tea.com.

...one mistake I see coffee retailers make when marketing tea is offering inexpensive teas that people can buy just about anywhere.

I firmly believe that if you serve great coffee you must also serve great tea. Don't panic. Tea does not have to complicate your life. If loose-leaf teas intimidate you, don't serve them. Offer tea bags instead. Many reputable companies sell unique and upscale tea bags, and you can charge a premium for them. Tea is an excellent item to have on your menu to attract those who don't drink coffee but still want to come to your coffee bar for a beverage and great ambiance.

Take tea seriously. Its cultivation, long history, how to store and serve it and how it's grown and processed can provide you with years of fascinating learning. The English are far ahead of us in understanding tea. And it's a large part of the culture in much of Asia.

I have attended the Take Me 2 Tea Expo (www.takeme2tea.com) in Las Vegas and I can attest to the fact that this industry is for real. It's growing with enthusiasm and passion, reminiscent of the specialty coffee industry ten years ago.

The number one mistake I see coffee retailers make when marketing tea is offering inexpensive teas that people can buy just about anywhere. With so many great teas available, don't offer the ordinary — offer the best. And have your employees try every one of them, so they can talk about various teas and how they taste. When you add tea, you will want to add tea training to your regular staff education.

All teas are grown in the tropical highlands. The leaves are picked by hand from bushes grown on sunny hillsides, usually by skilled women. Here is a brief primer on what you should know about the different types of tea. For more information, again visit www.planet-tea.com.

Though tea consumption has grown, total sales in coffee bars still represent only five to nine percent. Studies show teahouse customers prefer to linger longer, and subsequently spend less, which is probably why it's more difficult to do well serving only tea at a tea bar. The best way to make a profit from tea in your coffee bar is to select a range of interesting types not available in stores. Then learn about tea so you make the most of what you buy.

Great tea depends first on great tea leaves. Use filtered or spring water, never chlorinated, just as it reaches the boiling point. Green tea takes a lower temperature and some herbal teas need to simmer ten to twenty minutes. The standard measure is a teaspoon per person plus a teaspoon for the pot. Steep three to four minutes, though some need more, or less. If you want to be famous for the best, learn all you can about tea.

Varieties of Tea

Black Tea: To produce black tea, freshly picked green tea leaves are exposed to oxygen for several hours, which causes them to turn from green to almost black. The oxidation process is responsible for the hardy flavor associated with black tea.

Green Tea: In order to produce green tea, the oxidation process must be prevented, by either steaming or firing the green tea leaves. Green teas possess a more delicate flavor than black teas, and contain less caffeine. Green teas are becoming increasing popular due to their anti-oxidant properties and purported health benefits.

Oolong Tea: Oolong tea is a complex tea that is a cross between black and green leaves. To produce Oolong tea, the green tea leaves must be briefly exposed to the sun, which withers them. The leaves are then fired over charcoal, or pan-fried.

Herbal Tea: Herbal teas are not really teas — they contain no tea leaves. They are made from infusions of a variety of plants, roots, berries, seeds, peels and flowers. The huge variety of herbs prepared as infusions have been grown for centuries and many are used as remedies and tonics. Herbal teas contain no caffeine with the exception of yerba mate, which is popular in South America.

Smoothies and Meal–Replacement Drinks

Many coffee operations have developed sophisticated, yet simple, smoothies to cater to their health-conscious customers who love to drink their lunch. For those with children or for people who don't drink coffee or tea, smoothies are a welcome addition to a coffeehouse menu.

Keep your smoothie program simple. Select fruits that can be used in a number of different preparations. Give your smoothies special names. A "Raspberry 'Nana" may sell better than a "Raspberry and Banana Smoothie." Have fun with this product and use your blender to its full potential.

The Magic of Syrups

Flavored syrups have played an integral role in the growth of specialty coffee. In fact, I believe the industry would not have moved forward without them. It all started with the vision of the late Brandy Brandeburger, a retired employee of General Foods. By taking a cue from mixology, he believed the market for the espresso beverages served from carts in Seattle a dozen years ago could be expanded.

He experimented in his kitchen in Portland, Oregon with syrups made by Torani, one of the first companies in the syrup industry. He added flavors like hazelnut and vanilla to the lattes he made on his small home machine. He encouraged the new entrepreneurs of coffee to incorporate these flavors. Voilá: the signature drinks of specialty coffee were born. Since then, syrups have played a major role in most coffee operations worldwide.

Americans have become quite discriminating and many consumers are no longer satisfied with the commonplace. Today, many people are becoming aware of syrups' possibilities and are experimenting with different flavors in their local cafés. Many clients will choose a flavored latte over a standard brewed coffee.

Most suppliers offer 30 to 50 different syrup flavors to choose from. The flavors that generally sell best year-round are vanilla, hazelnut, Irish cream, and amaretto. Certain flavors enjoy seasonal popularity, and you should ask your suppliers for their advice and experiences concerning these. Berry flavors merchandise best in hot climates and in the summer months. In the winter months butter rum, eggnog and peppermint lead in popularity.

Specialty syrups on your retail shelves yield high profit margins and make a beautiful display. With proper lighting, the various colored bottles will achieve an almost neon allure in a product area. You'll need to educate yourself and your employees about the many uses of syrups, but if you experiment and get creative, you'll discover that gourmet flavored syrups are not just for coffee and sodas.

Many syrup brands come in two or three sizes. The smaller sizes will allow your customers to try different flavors at home for a minimal investment. Your espresso machine is the best way to introduce customers to flavors used creatively in your drinks. Other methods of marketing include in-store sampling, cross-merchandising, creating signature drinks, designing creative signage, printing bottleneck recipe cards, and offering the smaller bottles in coffee-based gift baskets.

You'll need to educate yourself and your employees about the many uses of syrups.

Frozen Iced Coffees and Other Gourmet Blended Drinks

In the past few years many companies have created great and easy-to-use products for use in your blender. In some areas a blender station can generate as much profit as an espresso machine if you offer the right menu items. Preparing blender drinks is usually as easy as opening a can and putting a scoop of gourmet powder or frappe mix into your blender with a shot of espresso or syrup. Be creative. Develop your own signature blender drinks. If you need help, look to your syrup and powder suppliers for ideas. Listed below are a few of the great syrup, chocolate, sauce and powder companies in our industry. Visit their Web sites or call for samples and recipes.

Syrup / Chocolate and Sauce Companies

Torani
www.torani.com
800.775.1925

Guittard Chocolate
www.guittard.com
800.468.2462

Monin
www.monin.com
727.461.3033

Stearns and Lehman
www.stearns-lehman.com
866.533.2722

DaVinci
www.davincigourmet.com
800.640.6779

Oscars
www.stearns-lehman.com/oscars.html
800.668.2833

Fabbri
www.fabbri1905.com
727.395.0483

Frozen Iced Coffee/Gourmet Powder/Frappe Mix Companies

Caffe D'Amore
www.caffedamore.com
800.999.0171

Cappuccine
www.cappuccine.net
800.511.3127

Big Train
www.bigtrain.com
800.244.8724

Dr. Smoothie
www.drsmoothie.com
714.449.9787

Potions in Motion
www.coffeeinventions.com
949.533.7461

Granita

Granita, an Italian invention, is a dense, high quality icy slush flavored with coffee, fresh fruit or a variety of syrups. Granita means "little granule." As the paddles in the cold machine roll through the liquid, tiny ice balls form. These give the drink a smooth and unique texture.

I am a firm believer in offering granita on a coffeehouse menu. One of the best things about granita is that it's easy to make. Simply add two bottles of syrup or granita mix to two gallons of water and let the machine do the rest. (Check with your supplier for the exact recipe.) It goes without saying that granita sells better in Florida than in Alaska. But during the spring, summer and fall months, granita sells well in most areas.

Older models of granita machines were prone to breakdowns, but today's machines are almost problem-free if cared for properly. Excellent and sophisticated granita machines cost about what some less expensive espresso machines do, so do your market research before you invest. Poll other operators. Is your climate right, your location, or your customer base? Do you have space for the equipment? Are you willing to do the marketing? Granita has a moderate food cost and a healthy profit margin, so you can often quickly earn back the money you invested in your machine and offer your customers a unique beverage option.

Gelato

More and more new coffee operations are offering gelato if space permits. Gelato is a highly flavored, superior frozen treat that appeals to children, adults, and coffee and non-coffee drinkers. If you're going to offer gelato, you'lll need to invest in a small display case and a machine if you want to make your own. If you are in a metro area, you may be able to find someone that makes gelato and have him or her deliver every few days. Gelato is served at most coffee bars in Italy for good reason — it puts extra dollars in the cash register during slow times of day such as the afternoon, and attracts customers who may never have entered your coffeehouse to buy coffee.

Adding Food

Offer customers something good to eat with their coffee, and soon they'll think of you when they feel hungry. In the morning, scones, muffins, bagels, rolls, croissants, toast, and even hot and cold cereals sell well. Fresh fruit and yogurt with granola is popular with the health conscious. Quick mix waffle batter, and a variety of toppings might work for you. Keep it simple. You aren't set up for home fries, ham and eggs. When you buy pre-made items, you can afford up to 50 percent in food costs because there's so little prep time.

If you offer only morning pastries, you are generating maximum revenue only in the morning. But at lunch you have to compete with restaurants. Don't let that discourage you. Again, keep it simple. Start with one or two pre-made soups that you cycle for predictable variety through the week, a couple of gourmet salads and consider a few items you can heat quickly in the microwave.

For quick salads, consider bagged mixed greens and a choice of dressing in single serving packets. Add meats, cheeses and nuts to make a simple salad into a special meal, served with baguette and butter. Prepare items in advance so it takes under two minutes to prepare a salad for serving.

Panini are cost-friendly little pre-made sandwiches kept chilled then grilled to order in about three minutes. Made on rustic breads or focaccia, the filling is minimal but of gourmet quality, and heating lets rich flavors permeate the bread. They taste great and are popular, piping hot, at breakfast or lunch with traditional or exotic ingredients. Panini are not yet overly common and can be prepared in advance.

If you're in the right area and open late, you can appeal to the after dinner and late night crowds. Offer desserts along with fine coffees and teas. When you can, and when it makes sense, offer fine wines and microbrew beers plus the most decadent treats in the area. Find the best maker of cakes, tortes and chocolate confections in your area and start with a small selection. Or you might set yourself apart as the place to go for gelato to die for, or parfait pleasures to melt the heart. All require little prep time, but definitely extra training of your staff.

More Ideas

Food service specialists can point you in the right direction. Provide them with information on your clientele and your business focus and they will guide you to appropriate products to fit your profile. Once you have chosen products to add, shape your menu with language that speaks to your customers and strengthens the identity of your business.

Attend trade shows and read coffee industry periodicals for information and ideas about the latest products. Keep your eyes open and stay on top of the latest beverage trends. If you can, attend at least one trade show a year. Walk the aisles and sample new products. A few years ago a new type of hot chocolate, similar to those produced in Italy, was introduced at a trade show. If you didn't taste it, you wouldn't have realized just how much different and better it was than the hot chocolate your mom made you as a child, encrusted with marshmallows.

...shape your menu with language that speaks to your customers and strengthens the identity of your business.

Again, search the pages of Specialty Coffee Retailer and Fresh Cup Magazine, retail-heavy periodicals that always feature cutting-edge products. Call companies that have new products and ask for samples, or, if the company has a representative in your area, ask him or her to show you the company's latest drink innovations.

Syrup, sauce, powder and liquid specialty drink companies always have people available to help you produce a great innovative product. In addition to marketing tips, these companies will supply you with great point-of-sale materials.

Along with menu items, every coffee bar can offer impulse buy treats such as chocolate covered coffee beans, mints, gourmet chocolate bars and coffee candies of all sorts. Specialty coffee candy suppliers are listed in trade journals.

Not every coffee operation should expand its menu to include all of the options I've mentioned above. For example, beer and wine may not fit into your mission statement or your location. However, I believe most operations should market tea. If you have a commercial blender in your operation, you should look very seriously at offering smoothies. Beverage menu options expand the number of people you can attract and will boost your bottom line.

CHAPTER 12

STORE LAYOUT AND AMBIANCE

The First Impression

Nothing is more important than a good first impression. The look and feel of your coffee bar conveys your business image and determines how your business is perceived. It's a crucial and highly important factor in marketing because it largely determines who will become your customer.

If your operation is poorly designed, either from the standpoint of ambiance or of working layout, your sales will suffer every day your doors are open. As surprising as it may sound, even small design deficiencies can impact your bottom line. Big design errors can actually prevent you from making a profit at all.

Use that first impression to be sure your customers see your operation as superior. Your design decisions must reflect your dedication to quality. The ambiance is a huge part of customer perception and is crucial to your overall marketing effort. Aim for design features that delight and make customers comfortable, to encourage them to come back, again and again.

Great ambiance doesn't just happen. It begins with a good layout.

Imagine a coffee bar with flower boxes and umbrella tables outside, where cheerful patrons sip iced drinks in the sunshine. Step in the door and intoxicating aromas beckon. Great colors, textures and lighting delight the eye. Fascinating merchandise is displayed in a prominent place. The perfect background music plays. Everything is sparkling clean, and the staff appears happy and busy.

Layout

Great ambiance doesn't just happen. It begins with good layout. You want a clear sense of welcome as people enter, with simple menus easy to read and understand. You want to serve people efficiently, especially during peak times.

If you've been in business for years and can't afford a remodel, try to view your operation from the customer's perspective to reveal low-cost changes that would facilitate better service. You want your design to help you serve each customer promptly even at your busiest times, while still making them feel relaxed and welcome. If you're not good at this sort of thing, ask a decorator or interior designer to do a walk-through and make comments.

Homework before Starting

If you are not yet open, study other stores and look at your unique merchandising needs while designing your store. Study the details. For example, make sure people lined up will have a good view of the pastries and deli case. Locate visually appealing items like granita machines in full view. Brightly colored granitas, turning in their cylinders, will catch your customers' eyes as they walk up to your counter. A granita machine tucked away where few will see the product will cost you sales.

Long before you sign any contracts with interior builders, look at your plans though the eyes of the customer. What do customers need? What makes things easy for them? For example, one of the biggest sources of confusion is where to place an order. You want your store to be customer-friendly, and an order counter near the front reduces the feeling of being lost as soon as you walk in. Good layout and rational traffic patterns are crucial to making everything work.

Strive to be original to set your coffee bar apart from your competition. Have a definite theme and concept in mind, before you begin. Planning for excellence begins with a rough draft of a concept that will set you apart.

You must transform you dreams and imagination into a clear sense of what you want, before you hire your experts. Do you want it bright or subdued, stark white, pastel or hot colors, open and spacious or broken up into cozy nooks? Do you want an Italian or Southwestern theme, cool sophistication or L.A. chic? Collect concepts, make a list of features and themes that fit your dreams, visit operations similar to what you envision and study and take notes on what you like and dislike there.

Of course, layout and design of your café will depend upon the amount of space you have, your customers and your theme. Work within the given limits, then aim to make your store the best.

Read books on how to design and lay out your coffee business. *Bean Business Basics*, Bellissimo's 670-page start-up/operational manual, devotes an entire chapter to proper coffeehouse design. Another Bellissimo book, *Opening a Specialty Coffee Drive-thru*, discusses design issues as they relate to a coffee drive-thru.

What have successful chain operations in your area done to make their stores unique? Often they have hired top designers to contribute to the design. Look at the colors they use and the art on their walls. Study their menu boards, tables, chairs, and stools. You should certainly duplicate certain aspects of what the chains have done well, but then opt for a design that creates a unique space to give your customers a special experience.

Design the Menu First

Your menu will determine what food-service equipment you'll need. Where will all this equipment be placed? Where is each task performed? Unless you have years of experience working in retail coffee, you'll never envision the hundreds of small considerations involved in design such as: Where will I prepare and stage my sandwich assembly? Where will I wash the lettuce and store my tomatoes? Will my baristas be able to pull shots and assemble drinks without colliding with an employee making iced drinks?

The basic rule is to design the back of your bar first.

The basic rule is to design the back of your bar first. Proper layout in this area is the key to good compact workflow so you can provide the service required and have happy employees, all of which will make your operation much more successful. Precision planning allows for the proper flow of work in the smallest area. This is important when you remember that only the square footage in the seating area generates profit.

Hire a Pro

Only a professional coffee bar design firm can understand all of the space and motion relationships that will make your operation work smoothly, well before any concrete is poured or any cabinets are built. Not every famous national design firm has experience in coffee café layout and few local firms have any at all.

A Florida client resisted my advice to contact a firm specializing in coffee bar design and spent several thousand dollars working with a local architect. After reviewing the plans, I recommended more than 30 changes. At that point, six weeks behind schedule, she realized she needed someone who specialized in coffee design. With the help of industry professionals, developing a winning food-service area, a great concept and ideal layout is easier than you might think. Hire pros and you won't have to build three coffee operations to finally get everything right.

Design Around your Theme

After the service areas, the next step is to design the front – the part of your operation where most of your in-store marketing will take place. Design this part of your operation with your theme in mind, recalling that your money will be made in the square footage in front of your workspace and counters.

Back to the Arizona retailer with the western theme. His store's layout perfectly complemented that theme and was comfortable for both tourists and the locals.

A western-style fence enclosed his retail area. He commissioned a local artist to paint a large mural on one of the walls. The seating area was extensive. Through large windows, customers could sit and watch the tourists strolling down the street. An area in the back provided enough privacy to allow local business people to meet.

Years ago, Bellissimo worked with a retailer in Hawaii who operated a large kiosk in the middle of an outdoor mall frequented by tourists. She chose a theme representative of the big island of Hawaii. In keeping with this theme, we helped her design a watertight roof covered with thatch and hired a builder to cut long stocks of bamboo in half length-wise to use in constructing a fence around the kiosk. She carried her theme throughout her menu, giving her beverages special names that evoked old Hawaii. Her employees dressed in traditional Hawaiian clothing to further create the ambiance she wanted to convey.

Design for Comfort

Unless you have a small operation in a downtown metropolitan area where 95 percent of your sales are to-go drinks, you will need to design your café to accommodate customers who want to linger. A good "third place" will have attractive and comfortable seating.

The coffee bar in my Portland neighborhood is a great example of how to create an inviting space for customers to spend time. As you enter, two couches and two chairs provide plush comfort for those who plan to stay awhile and lounge.

The seating area is large, with numerous tables. If a big group should stop in, the operator allows customers to push tables together to create enough table surface for the entire party. Two-top tables in the back allow for more privacy if customers are interested in a more intimate setting. In the front of the coffee bar, stools face a wall, a nice touch if someone is drinking a cup of coffee alone and just wants to read the newspaper or go online.

Chains employ experts to position retail items at key points in their stores.

The most unique seating arrangement I have ever seen was at a friend's coffee bar in the Midwest. I thought what she did was pure genius. She designed a large table in the shape of an oversized half surfboard and attached it to the wall. The table had ten or twelve stools around it, and almost everyone who took a seat there had come in alone. She left newspapers and magazines on the table, but the configuration encouraged people to interact with each other, so these publications often went unread. If these customers had each taken their own table, they probably wouldn't have made an effort to start a conversation. The group atmosphere created by this unusual table resulted in many new friendships. In addition, the table often prevented two-tops from being used by only one customer. Brilliant!

Design the Retail Area

If you are going to sell merchandise, you will need to create a retail area that fits into your overall design. Chains employ experts to position retail items at key points in their stores, so before you add retail items scrutinize how they do this. You can be sure they have spent hundreds of thousands of dollars to study the merchandising aspect of the business. Pay attention to the way successful coffee bars and large chain stores integrate retail into their floor plan. Ask yourself how practical your display will be. Will your bulk teas, T-shirts and other retail items be in clear view of your cashier to prevent theft?

Interior Finishes

You don't need to spend a million dollars to build a great coffee bar. One of Bellissimo's clients installed a floor of inexpensive fiberboard covered with transparent gym coat. It was stunning. Another practical flooring option is acid-etched concrete. The new high-traffic, commercial vinyl tiles come in a variety of slate patterns and colors, are long wearing, easy to lay and very inexpensive. Quality non-slip ceramic tile is expensive but lasts longer than other choices, with minimal care. Choose patterns that camouflage soil.

Avoid carpets as they soil quickly, are hard to clean and need to be replaced all too frequently. Hardwood floors require care and can warp if exposed to moisture. Mats near the entry keep floors cleaner. The kick guard at the counter, about five inches high, can be of rubber that coordinates with your color scheme.

If your operation is in an older or historic building, leave the walls in their natural state if they are in good condition. Old brickwork, cleaned up, is beautiful. Aged wood has a unique appeal. You can camouflage ductwork or paint it bright colors to make a statement. Dark ceilings work well in large spaces, while small spaces feel much more open with bright ceilings.

We've found that in general the lighter earthy colors work best for walls. Study decorating books for ideas. Wall treatments such as murals, wainscoting, wall textures, faux finishes or decorated borders add a distinctive touch.

Ergonomics

Ergonomics, or human engineering, is about making the designed environment fully compatible with people. Ergonomics was originally the domain of industrial efficiency experts. It's the science of the design of devices, systems and working conditions to match the requirements of the human body. It talks about how workers move through their tasks and how to make it easy for them to do their best.

Good ergonomic design will allow your staff to do things with the fewest steps and the least reaching, performing their jobs quickly without colliding with others or creating hazards. Good ergonomics will increase convenience, raise efficiency and reduce wasted effort. Use ergonomics to maximize safety and help prevent accidents, while reducing frustration and fatigue, and increasing staff comfort.

Good ergonomics is also design that respects your customers. Today, it includes an understanding of how chairs and tables and counters fit, how people line up, how they view signage and how long they will enjoy sitting in a particular chair. Let ergonomics help you achieve the best fit for your service counter, seating areas, coffee displays, pastry cases and more.

Lighting

Maximize natural light, but think about the consequences. With all the heat generated by your machines and people, sunny windows and skylights can put an extra load on your cooling system. The most effective way to shade big windows is with an outside awning to block direct sunshine before it gets to the glass. Use interior drapery, shades or shutters as needed, to cut direct sunlight or to keep the heat inside during very cold weather.

Lighting design is crucial to your operation. Bluish fluorescent light and shiny surfaces can assault the senses. Colored incandescent bulbs and mini-halogen track lighting create a much warmer environment. Provide some areas bright enough for reading, and other areas where the light is subdued so customers can relax.

Lighting is a complex art form and new technology is rapidly evolving. Study lighting design books and magazines for ideas, but don't try to come up with a lighting plan yourself. Power usage, safety and security, mood, color, and other considerations enter into good lighting design decisions. Talk with lighting experts before you make your choices.

Seating

Is your business a coffeehouse where people will come to relax with friends? You'll want soft couches and chairs with low coffee tables. Or is it a high-volume coffee bar where people make a brief visit and are content with tall, high stools or hard chairs that are easy to keep clean? Small, hard chairs encourage shorter stays.

Offer many seating options. Large commercial restaurant wholesalers will have the best choices. Be sure that the chairs you choose can be repaired, repainted or replaced when they wear out. Look for good back support and chair heights that work well with your tables. Bring a couple of critical friends along and try out every piece of furniture you're considering.

Look for tables that are easy to clean and of a finish compatible with your design and theme. We've found that tables 32 inches high are ideal, comfortable for most people and chairs fit well. Some table styles allow height adjustments. A black base is simple to touch up with paint when it gets scuffed.

Internet

Today, most coffeehouses offer wireless Internet connections. Most also offer plugs to power laptop computers and save battery power. At almost every coffee business I walk into, I see numerous people working on laptops or surfing the Internet as they sip their favorite drinks. This technology, like others, is changing rapidly. Choosing a service provider can be a difficult decision. Be sure you keep up with the latest technology.

Music

Plan for music from day one. If you intend to have a good music system, the wiring has to be installed before the sheet rock and wall coverings go on. And you need to make decisions about where to keep the CD player and the disks and plan procedures for who will be changing them.

> The type of music you play will often dictate the mood of your customers...

Music is a crucial part of your ambiance. The type of music you play will often dictate the mood of your customers and what kind of customer walks through your doors, and who walks out. Be sure staff appreciates the fact that the music is not for their entertainment, but for the pleasure of the customers.

If you don't know much about music, find someone to help you select a background sound that creates the atmosphere you want for your business. The music you play in early morning may be very different than what you play at noon or in the late evening with wine and dessert.

Perfection in the Simple Touches

To help you design your business, buy books from the Martin Pegler series, with pictures of hundreds of cafés from around the world (these books are available from Bellissimo). When we work with our clients at Bellissimo, we advise them to look through these books and tell us what they like about particular designs. Most of these clients like certain aspects of four or five different operations. The educated client with strong ideas gets the best work from the design professional. By doing your own research, you help your consultant or professional designer hone in on what is important to you and on the feeling you want to convey in your operation.

...there is no reason you can't create a one-of-a-kind coffee operation.

With limitless design options, there is no reason you can't create a one-of-a-kind coffee operation. You may decide to acid-etch your floors in four colors. Floor to ceiling drapery down one of your walls can create a quiet and peaceful ambiance. Local art that changes each month can provide ambiance and an added income source. Murals can transport your customers to a different place or time. Let your imagination and that of friends and professionals lead you to create a setting that is attractive, comfortable, workable, unique and very profitable.

The design of your work areas determines how well your staff can function. The image projected by your design decisions will create your store's atmosphere. It's difficult to measure or even to define, but everyone who comes in can feel it. When the atmosphere is enticing, comforting, exciting or fun it draws people into the store and enriches their experience, making them want to return.

CHAPTER 13

THE IMPORTANCE OF BRANDING AND IDENTITY

A number of years ago, a friend of mine named Robert was preparing to open a unique Italian bistro. He had two good friends who were "part-time artists" and was considering having one of them create the logo design. One would charge him a few hundred dollars, and the other would trade a design for some free meals. He asked me how much I thought he should spend on developing a logo. I told him using either friend could be a tragic mistake, one he would regret for years. I recommended a skilled designer in town who quoted him a price of $1500 for the job. After some discussion, he went with the professional.

Robert told me several years later that initially he felt he had spent too much on branding, but came to realize the logo was worth much more than the $1500 he'd spent. During the years he owned his business, many customers complimented him on the logo, describing it as "cool" and "cutting-edge." Robert used his logo in his television advertising as well as on hats and T-shirts. That logo became a well-known symbol in the community.

You Need a Pro

People know who you are by what they see. Perception is everything. That's why your business image is vital to your success, a continual part of your marketing effort that affects every part of your operation. Like Robert, you need a design professional who can produce a unique, cool, cutting-edge logo. You also want it to be memorable and to convey a business image that motivates trust and loyalty in the people you want as customers.

Today, you may have to spend $1000 to $5000 for a professional logo and business image package that includes all your needed graphics. It's worth every penny. This will be your identity. If it doesn't look professional, customers will have a hard time believing that any part of your business is professional. You will be competing against major chains that do a first-rate job of presenting the best possible appearance. Learn from what they have done.

A business that invests in an effective logo may determine, as Robert did, that was some of the wisest money they spent. The graphic image sets the tone even when the venture is still in the planning stages. It tells all your suppliers you're serious. It earns the respect of product reps and other professionals in your home community. It allows you to feel pride in everything associated with your enterprise. A bad or so-so logo can undercut your self-esteem and work against you every time it appears.

What is Branding?

Your logo may be the main focus of your advertising, and can provide a common visual link for all other design decisions, from products to packaging to special events and marketing communications. The brand works when it conveys at a glance what you represent, and shows up on everything associated with your operation, from your business cards to the labels on your sugar packets and nametags on employee aprons. Your menu, handouts, ads, signage, paper products, gift items and more will all incorporate your identity in the form of your name, tag line and logo.

You want your business "brand" to be instantly recognized and positioned in your marketplace, and to project a clear identity that everyone associates with you. One of the most important things you can project in your marketing is a strong, appealing brand image. Creativity is the key to a strong brand identity that reflects your business personality.

To begin the branding process, start with your positioning strategy, defining how you want people to perceive your coffee bar. Identify your market niche, the people you'll cater to and their needs and wants. Speak to that group. Don't make the mistake of trying to market to everyone. As a small business, you don't need everyone. But you need to set yourself apart from the big chains. Choose one or two related niches. Near a college, you have to appeal to bright young adults and also campus employees. Downtown, your market is business people and office workers. Every marketing effort has to be the right message, aimed at the right customers.

You want your business "brand" to be instantly recognized and positioned in your marketplace.

Take the time to choose a great, evocative name. Next, envision an image or logo that works with that name. Finally, create a tag line, a short sentence that describes who you are or what you stand for. For example, I named one of my first coffee bars "Caffe Primavera." In Italian, "Primavera" means springtime. For my logo I used a Corinthian column with a floral theme at its base, surrounded by two Renaissance angels. The tag line was "Coffee delivered from heaven."

I have seen many small companies make the mistake of choosing an identity too quickly. Sometimes Bellissimo arrives to train a retailer on-site, having not worked with them previously. Often, the first thing we see is a sign with a poorly designed logo. We do our best to explain how to use these ill-conceived logos, but to be honest, if the identity is not professionally designed, do you want to see it everywhere you look?

If you're a new operation, have your design professional help you conceive and execute your branding program and assist you with your marketing, unifying all your visuals from the sign on your store to the graphics on your Web site. If you are an existing establishment and feel you made poor choices when developing your brand, you may want to consider re-branding. However, this can prove costly, and may not make sense, especially if your business is well established. But even established companies re-brand from time to time if their name and logo has a dated and worn look or feel. Betty Crocker has had a number of different faces and costumes in her long history.

Noteworthy Examples

Inspired branding defines the coffee world. Seattle's Caffé D'arte (Italian for "coffee of art") uses a simple logo that incorporates the company name and a cup in a design of traditional Italian colors. Its tag line is "Taste the Difference." The brand indicates this company has traditional Italian coffee and suggests a high quality product.

Another Seattle coffee company with impressive branding is Caffé Vita. Its logo features an Italian clown holding a cup. The image is classy, whimsical and reminds me of Carnival in Venice, reinforcing the link to Italy, the Mecca of espresso. The company uses its name and branding in fun and unique ways, probably more so than any other company in the industry.

Once the company gave away black hats with an embroidered logo that simply said "Caffé Vita." But for the younger crowd, as a very creative promotion, the company produced cheap black and white foam baseball hats that from a distance read "VITA SUCKS." Upon closer inspection, you could read small print that said, "VITA is great! What SUCKS is when you can't find any!"

When you are developing your identity, first define your target or niche market and make sure your branding speaks to those groups. For example, if you are located close to a university or college, your branding should appeal to the young adults who will probably be your main source of income. If you're in a suburban shopping mall, you will probably want to develop an identity that will engage mothers, shoppers and other area residents.

Your Name

Creating a strong name is important because it's what will draw customers in and what they will remember and tell their friends. Your name will be on all your signage, on your business cards, letterhead, checks, mugs, and more. Make it a great name. The name you choose should fit three criteria.

Unique — it will catch the attention of your target market and stand out from the crowd.

Fitting — It will be consistent with your concept and image. Don't call your coffeehouse The Fishmarket, even if it's near the docks.

Easy to Remember — When someone asks a customer where she got the wonderful coffee served at a party, you want her to recall your name. Keep it simple — three words maximum. One word is easiest to remember.

Your Logo

A logo works when it conveys your goals and represents you as having high credibility. Credibility means your message is more likely to be heard and seen. A powerful logo is contemporary and very simple, yet it will symbolize how you operate and will characterize your attitudes. Research shows that if your logo says you are forward-thinking, competent and reliable, all the messages you put out, associated with this logo, will be accepted by the receiver. The challenge in the coffee business is that you want people to trust you as the passionate expert on coffee and also want the logo to tell people you are fun and dedicated to pleasure.

> **A powerful logo is contemporary and very simple.**

Your Tag line

A tag line is your unique description. It conveys to customers the special benefit you offer them, a reason to choose you over the competition. Domino's tag line is "Fresh hot pizza in thirty minutes or less." They don't claim to have exotic gourmet pizza. They claim it's fresh, hot and fast. People want to know what's in it for them. Your tag line should convey what they will get from you. It's not necessarily your marketing slogan, but rather a fundamental positioning statement that sets the standard for your business.

You can't overestimate the importance of a great tag line in your marketing program. Here are some fictional examples: Albany Coffee: "Your Hometown Roaster," and Anchorage Coffeehouse: "Hot Brews for a Cold Day." Your tag line should tell your customers what your mission is in one short, easily remembered concise statement.

The typeface you choose for your name, logo and other graphics is a subtle but extremely important form of communication. Unless you have a lot of experience with typefaces, this will be a difficult call for you, one more reason to choose a professional to create your image.

Testing

All aspects of your branding are best tested before you adopt them. Spend an afternoon talking with people who fit the profile of your target market. Stop them as they walk by your site and ask them what they think of the tentative name, logo, tag line and typefaces you've chosen. Or you can interview them in the lunchroom of the nearby college. Avoid questions with simple answers such as, "Which of these two do you like best?" The ideal way to get their impression is with an open question such as, "What does this make you think of?"

A good rule is to have as many people as possible look at your prospective logo and other branding concepts before you invest any money. Don't bother asking personal friends and relatives, unless they actually fit your target market. This is not an exercise in winning approval but a serious research effort to see if you're on the right track. Once you've committed to a business image, the cost of mistakes and of changing your mind is extremely high. You're on the right track when people in the target market group are giving responses like, "It makes me think of taking home some fresh roasted beans to brew up a pot of great coffee for my friends."

Why Branding is Important

Your brand is more than an image and a series of words, it's your identity. Your name and logo should say something about you to people who have never been to your establishment. It has to be strong enough to convey a message and a feeling in an instant. When you run a small newspaper ad, your logo may be all someone has by which to judge your business. An appealing, professional logo alone may be a reason to visit your coffee establishment for the first time.

Properly executed branding can set small chains and independent retailers apart from the big chains. A small chain in Portland specializing in organic, shade-grown, fair-trade and relationship coffee has created branding with thematic ties to its niche market. It appeals to coffee consumers interested in the social issues surrounding coffee. So its branding is colorful and fun, with an International and ecological flavor, suggesting an affinity with the environment and sustainability issues.

Comply with the Law

Taste may be subjective but the law is less so. From a legal standpoint, it's extremely important to check with your attorney before finalizing your name, to avoid choosing one already claimed. In many states, you simply call a state office to find out which business names are already registered, choose one not taken, then pay a fee to protect your own name. Every state has different laws regarding business names. A client of mine in Arizona wanted to register the name "Caffe Paradiso," but because there was already a "Paradise Café" in the state, my client was unable to use the name. In other states, the name may have been acceptable. Make sure you follow the proper registration procedures in your state so you won't have to change your name years later because of an infringement.

> Taste may be subjective but the law is less so.

Consistency

Consistent use of your image is vital to a credible business image. The first time a distorted logo or misspelled tag line phrase or wrong color shows up on a T-shirt or in an ad, you'll wish you'd set up rules to assure consistency.

Every large and successful organization has clear guidelines and insists on everyone following rules for how and where their name, logo and tag line are to be used. You can do the same thing. Be sure everyone using your logo for any purpose gets a copy of these rules, and you should review any designs for compliance.

Logo Items

If you have a great logo and brand, you can add another profit center to your business by selling retail logo items. The sale of retail merchandise means selling your ad to people who will give it exposure. That puts additional dollars in your till every day. But it only works if your brand is visually appealing and cool.

Logo items you can sell include:
- T-shirts / Sweatshirts
- Mugs / Coasters
- Thermal mugs
- Branded pre-sold coffee cards
- Hats
- Chocolates
- Frisbees
- Key chains

These may cost a little bit to produce, but selling retail merchandise emblazoned with your branding amounts to free advertising. To encourage purchase, many establishments sell this type of retail item at a small markup. Even if you only make a dollar on a T-shirt, the true value lies in the marketing bang you get by having people promoting your product outside of your store. Wherever your logo appears, add a small TM as evidence that your trademark is registered. Paper to-go cups with your logo that employees take back to an office are great advertising. If you can't afford to have them pre-printed, use stickers. The point is always think of the residual effects that your branding can have on your business.

Image Ads

Ralph Lauren, Calvin Klein, Chanel and other fashion marketers often use ads illustrating a lifestyle concept. "The Bold Look of Kohler" sells upscale plumbing fixtures in fantasy settings. A romantic photograph or film clip of gorgeous people enjoying life to the fullest conveys the lush image of grand possibilities that these brands want you to associate with their products. No specific product, price or offer is presented. With a local coffee business and a clear focus on who your customers are, you can do some image ads too. Be bold, brazen, sensuous or funny and people will remember you.

Branding and identity are two of the most important parts of your overall marketing program. Your marketing materials and every part of your business will incorporate its elements. Think hard, take your time and hire a professional to create an image that combines credible and cool, expertise and romance. Money spent on a professional business identity is money well invested.

CHAPTER 14

CROSS MARKETING AND PARTNERING

A few years back the owner of a very successful pizza operation, on an island in the Caribbean, hired Bellissimo to assist him in opening a coffee business. I had been impressed with this client's passion during the many phone conversations we'd had leading up to our initial meeting. His intention was to do everything right. He was determined to spare no expense in creating a beautiful operation and offering the best quality products.

My associate and I arrived late in the evening and our client met us at the airport, intent upon ushering us straight to our hotel and waiting to show us his nearly completed coffee operation in the morning. But curiosity got the best of us, so we asked if we could take a quick look that night.

Picturing the island, I had imagined a tropical paradise complete with swaying palm trees, pristine beaches and maybe even a monkey or two. The reality, however, was far from my vision. At first glance, the island appeared poverty stricken. The farther we drove, the more abandoned cars I saw next to homes built of unpainted cinderblocks.

I was told the most upscale store on the island was similar to Kmart, and I immediately had doubts about the viability of our client's project. Would islanders want, or be able to afford, a $3 latte or a slice of the expensive frozen Italian cheesecake that our client planned to import from New York City?

We drove deeper and deeper into the island, and the longer we were on the road, the more worried I became. We were traveling on narrow lanes surrounded by destitution. I smiled when I saw signs for a speed limit of 35 mph. The potholes in the road were so bad that not even a Hummer could have gone faster than that.

Upon arrival, I was certain we were in an area no tourist would ever visit. It was little more than a pit stop of a few hundred residents. Besides my client's pizza operation, the retail district included a bank, a utility company and a couple of strip malls housing a tire business and an auto parts store.

It seemed likely that the local people would spend money on our client's pizza, given its universal appeal, but I doubted they would buy anything but inexpensive brewed coffee from an upscale coffee bar. Obviously the client didn't share any of my reservations. The coffee bar was stunning, upscale with a true Caribbean feel. In the midst of the impoverishment, the coffeehouse boasted small, hand-crafted tin roofs covering the entire bar area. The decor was of soothing, pastel colors that complemented the indigenous artwork.

What took us by surprise was the ingenuity of our client. He had cut a grand, arching opening in the wall between the coffee bar and his pizza business next door so people could easily walk from one business to the other. In theory, this was a perfect example of cross marketing. But I still had doubts and some serious concerns. Was this too fashionable? Would the decor and pricing prove intimidating to the locals?

Pizza and Coffee

Through the process of opening this operation, we experienced cross marketing, hands on. During the busy lunch hour, when the pizza operation was packed with locals, employees distributed coupons for the coffee bar.

Taster trays of granita drinks and iced mochas were sampled for the pizza crowd. We took to the streets, dispersing printed menus with a phone number, to shop owners in the area. We included personalized messages that invited them to phone in to-go orders that would be ready when they arrived.

Within a few days the coffee bar was packed with people. Customers purchased the sampled products by the dozens. We offered samples of the upscale pastries in the pizza operation, and soon many of the pizza customers came over to the coffee bar for dessert.

...you don't have to own another business next-door or even down the street to utilize cross marketing successfully.

As the coffee operation flourished, our client gave out small samples of his pizza to customers, some who had never tried his pizza. Not only did he hit a home run with his coffee bar, but he also noticed that his pizza operation was showing a double-digit increase in sales. Cross marketing helped both of these operations thrive.

This was a real story of success. But you don't have to own another business next-door or even down the street to utilize cross marketing successfully. Any good entrepreneur can and should do it on a continual basis.

Cross Marketing a New or Existing Business

It's never too early to start cross marketing your business. During your construction phase, get to know your neighborhood and introduce yourself and your concept to area businesses. Pass out coupons to local storeowners and discuss ways in which you can build up each other's customer bases.

Inexpensive postcards are a great way to advertise your business. If possible, tap your staff for someone with creative ability and have them help you produce a hip design for the card. On the back, add your location, hours and perhaps news of a special discount. Suggest helping your neighboring businesses use similar programs. You can position their promotional materials on your counter or in a rack and have them do the same with yours.

> If you don't know what's actually working, you have gained no control over the success of future cross-marketing promotions in your area.

If your business is already in operation, use a similar approach and distribute discount cards to neighboring merchants. It's important to make them feel special and a part of your coffee business. If they love your coffee and feel comfortable in your coffee bar, they'll encourage their friends and customers to patronize your business, as well.

An offer of free coffee through cross promotions has proven to be one of the fastest ways to build a customer base. The idea is to provide coupons for customers of businesses with similar clientele. The other business has a "gift" to offer their customers and you get a new person visiting your shop.

Run no more than a couple of promotions at a time, to be sure you are not overwhelmed by a rapid rise in numbers. Keep careful records of the origin of coupons turned in to you, so you know which nearby businesses are good cross marketing partners for you. If you don't know what's actually working, you have gained no control over the success of future cross-marketing promotions in your area.

Partnering

You're probably familiar with the concept of partnering, but may not have applied it to your coffee business. Make a list of businesses near yours with similar target markets. You and these people have common interests and clients. Meet with the owner or manager of, for example, a nearby video store and suggest ideas for synergy with programs that suit each business.

If you wish to cater to the top income levels you might want to link up with expensive car dealerships, an exclusive spa or salon, the gourmet wine and cheese shop or an upscale jeweler. How about advertising links, sharing the cost of a four-color brochure, and sharing mailing lists? You could work with retail partners to create gift baskets featuring products and coupons from numerous businesses.

In Eugene, Oregon, to fight the chains a group of upscale local businesses have joined forces under the heading of Unique Eugene. They emphasize excellence and originality. By joining forces, they can afford to produce large professional ads for print and electronic media, promoting the special products and great service they alone can offer.

We have a Coffeehouse in this Town?

On a consulting job in a small Wyoming town that has often been compared to towns like Aspen, Colorado, I expected an inviting market for a specialty coffee or tea business. Many thousands of tourists visit this town each year to wander through the fashionable galleries and boutiques and the numerous antique stores that line the streets.

I arrived a day early. My client was the owner of a coffeehouse that had failed to turn a significant profit. I had planned on spending that first day as a tourist, but my concern for my client did not allow me to take a leisurely day off. The client had hired me to find out why his coffee bar — one of the most beautiful I had ever seen — was not profitable. I wanted to start my investigation as soon as possible.

I spent the day on the main street and visited every single business. I asked each shop owner, "Is there a place in town to get one of those espresso drinks, you know, like a latte or cappuccino?" I was shocked when almost every single shop owner said, "No."

Then I said I had heard there was a place to get espresso and told them the name. Fewer than a dozen people in other businesses knew of the operation. It was immediately apparent why this coffee operation was struggling. If the local business people didn't know it even existed, how could they possibly patronize it or recommend it to their customers?

We developed a campaign to inform the local merchants about the coffee business. We knew we had to offer them something in return for helping us promote the coffee bar. So part of our plan was to choose an employee who had an outgoing and genuine personality to pass out a "local card" to every downtown merchant in order to make them feel like part of a special community. The card was good for a 15 percent discount each time they used it.

Since the town's business district is made up of mostly antique and gift stores, we developed a flyer to hand out to the coffee bar's customers listing interesting businesses that our coffee-seeking visitors might want to patronize. The campaign was very successful and, of all the suggestions I made, this was the one that was the most helpful in increasing sales.

I have rarely been as impressed as I was the day I walked into this client's coffeehouse. The ambiance was perfect and the retail section was colorful and creative. But without good marketing, added to the other essentials like a knowledgeable staff and the perfect cup of java, it would have been impossible for the business to be successful.

Become More Integrated in Your Community

When devising ways to help another business or group, think outside of the box. For example, sponsor an auction for a good cause, and make sure they mention the name of your business. A civic center or local theater can benefit from having you promote them and in turn, maybe they can help you. You may only be listed in a "Thank You" section they publish in the program or the local paper after the event, but the listing of your business' name will demonstrate your involvement. It shows you care about the town in which you live.

In the summertime, you might want to look into local outdoor events. You can promote a cultural festival and serve your coffee at a weekend event. Consider sponsoring a Little League team. Use this opportunity to let the group know you support them with your presence, and use the opportunity to distribute coupons and flyers.

Contact radio stations and offer to bring by free coffee to the morning show each day or to any live remote broadcast. It's highly likely that they will mention your name dozens of times, for the cost to you of a gallon of gas and a pound of coffee.

Because of the normally small ticket amount, running a specialty coffee business is very much a numbers game. You need to do everything possible to gain new customers on a continuous basis. Cross marketing will work whether your business is in a small village in the middle of a tropical island or in midtown Manhattan. A promotional maneuver can help any business grow and attract more customers. Cross marketing will without a doubt make you a much more integrated part of your business community. As you help others, they will in turn help you. Remember the adage – the more you give, the more you will receive.

CHAPTER 15

PROMOTIONS AND SPECIAL EVENTS

Take a close look at any retail establishment in the world. It doesn't matter whether you are browsing a street bazaar in Mexico City or window-shopping at Saks Fifth Avenue in New York. In almost every retail setting you'll see something on sale or an item that the business is promoting. Retail businesses advertise items or put them on sale for many reasons. Often it is because the item is not selling well or may be out of season. Or it may be the newest product that is promoted, something unique and cutting edge that the retailer hopes will attract new patrons.

The goal is increased sales. By planning in advance for a specific promotion or sales event, you can maximize your results. Come up with some ideas related to a holiday, Mother's or Father's Day, or Valentine's Day for example, and build a promotion around that. Design an action calendar, inform your employees, prepare signage, set aside appropriate amounts of product, run ads if needed and you're on your way to a seasonal sales event that will increase your bottom line.

Your Drink Specials

Most of your promotions will probably involve drink specials. After all, you're in the business of selling coffee, not retail items. So focus on what you do best, selling great coffee, and market your special beverages in creative and innovative ways.

Not every promotion is a limited time event.

Leading up to Valentine's Day, you could have a two-for-one special on a coffee drink. How about a free "Latte for Your Lover?" Cupid's Cappuccino or Lover's Latte, with red sprinkles might be a hit. You could offer a special blend of beans on sale for all members of your bean club. With promotions such as this you may have lots of new people sign up for a club membership, providing you with the valuable demographic data you need for adjunct marketing projects.

Create seasonal gift displays on your retail shelves to encourage impulse buys of higher priced items. Offer gift cards with your logo if you learn this purchase is a gift. Decorate the store for the holiday, inside and outside. Display signage advertising your specials. Come up with seasonal theme ideas for many holidays and make plans well in advance for creative ways to promote them.

Your Regular Specials

Not every promotion is a limited time event. Some are an ongoing part of your business and part of why your coffee bar is special. Every coffee operation should develop a menu of "Signature Drinks" with names that are distinctive to the theme of the operation. For example, when I opened my first coffee operation, Primavera, it was the first coffee bar in the area to have an Italian theme. Primavera had four drink specials that in essence were flavored lattes or mochas. I gave the specials the following names: The Milano, The Venezia, The Verona, and The Siena.

In each of my specials, I added a shot of gourmet syrup or chocolate, or both. The Milano was a white mocha with a shot of hazelnut syrup. In The Venezia, I used dark chocolate and macadamia nut syrup. Each of my specials had a distinctive flavor that appealed to a variety of customers.

If a customer ordered a regular large-size mocha with a shot of syrup, he would pay $3 for the mocha and .50¢ for the syrup, or $3.50. If he bought one of my signature drinks, he would pay $2.95 for basically the same drink. My business was located across the street from a hospital, and two of my regular customers were nurses. Once I heard one of them say, "I love the Milano. I get it everyday." Her friend replied, "I never get anything but the Verona. I'm hooked on that drink."

People love to have their own special drinks. Based on my own experience, I can tell you that people often order the same beverage day after day. From time to time, give away samples of your special drinks to encourage people to discover something new. You may be able to get one of your brewed coffee drinkers, who normally spends a $1.50 a day at your coffee bar, to start drinking a large iced mocha that costs $3.50.

Daily and Weekly Specials
I believe you need to mix things up a bit. If you sell bulk or bagged beans, run a special on a different origin coffee each week, or at least each month. In addition, you can market this same coffee as your "Coffee of the Week." You can link this to special discounts for bean club members.

In addition to my standard signature drinks I promoted a "Coffee of the Week" such as Guatemalan Antigua, and a "Coffee of the Month" like Ethiopian Harrar. Give people the opportunity to taste and learn about origin coffees, and how much labor and pride small growers invest in great coffee. This will expand their knowledge of the world and encourage them to be adventurous and try what they might consider an exotic coffee instead of ordering the usual "House Blend."

Marketing and promoting special coffees is part of your effort to educate your clients to appreciate the richness and variety of available coffee products. When you educate your customers' palates, you also generate greater bean sales. And as you become known for your expertise and what you teach your customers, they will recognize your business as unique because you may be offering something your competition doesn't.

When you educate your customers' palates, you also generate greater bean sales.

Vary your specials from season to season. In the summer, offer lots of cold drink specials. During the Christmas season, many cafés offer peppermint and eggnog lattes. As I stated in an earlier chapter, one of the large chains attributes increased profits to promoting a new beverage nearly every quarter. Because you are more flexible than a huge corporation, you can do this also and in a shorter time frame if you desire.

Seasonal Promotions

Run in-store specials for each season. Christmas is a perfect time to bring in additional gift items. Most retailers buy their Christmas stock in July. So shop early to get the items you want. Many unique items sell out quickly, and if you decide in late October to buy stock for mid November, you may be too late. If you offer coffee jewelry, it may not sell well in July, but may do very well in November and December.

Holidays such as Christmas, Valentine's Day, Mother's Day, Thanksgiving, Halloween, and Easter are all great opportunities to promote gift baskets. Purchase attractive baskets from a wholesaler. Or some creative person on your staff may want to make up some from products you stock. Items to include are brewers, syrups, coffees, teas, chocolates and maybe even a book on coffee.

As I mentioned earlier, it has become commonplace for retailers to sell eggnog lattes during Christmas holiday season, Thanksgiving to New Year's Day. However, you couldn't give these drinks away in June. Be creative with your syrups and offer seasonal beverages that include fruit syrups in summer. Amazing new flavors are created each year, like watermelon, kiwi or mango.

Your Retail Items

Unlike some retailers, coffee businesses don't usually stock seasonal items that will need to be put on clearance after a particular holiday. However, you may have purchased a large number of a certain brewer that didn't sell as well as you expected. If this is the case, you might want to put them on sale at just above cost. Use those break-even dollars to purchase new stock.

Most likely, you'll have special items that you want to promote. For example, if you want to sell more French presses, announce an upcoming evening class on how to use this brewing device. Or, you might find a home-brewing device at a trade show and hold a class on its unique qualities, thus introducing people to exciting and interesting new technology. Offer a special on the product you promote during the week prior and after the class, selling them at, say, only 25 percent above cost to any customer who attends the class and purchases a pound of coffee at the same time.

Be Present at Special Events

Use every opportunity to promote your coffee business in the community. If there is an annual summer event, ask the organizers how you can participate, either with a cart or a small booth. Can you arrange to have a presence at the county fair, festival, outdoor concert series or any local event? While there, distribute lots of advertisements and flyers on your specials to the thousands of people in attendance who may come into your retail store for the first time at a later date because of your promotional effort.

I know of many retailers who sell their coffee in athletic stadiums or performing arts centers. You can make a sizeable profit doing this, but even if your profits are marginal, the value of exposing new people to your product makes it worthwhile. My friend in the Midwest serves her coffee at art openings, and I doubt she makes any direct profit. But as a result, her coffeehouse has become a daily stop for many in the arts community.

In-Store Events

In addition to classes designed to introduce and sell equipment, if you have the space, hold other in-store training or educational events in your store. Show a film on a Saturday morning like "The Passionate Harvest" and discuss it with attendees afterward. Run specials on the coffees they just viewed picked and harvested, in the film.

In-store trainings are a win-win situation.

Many of your customers don't know how to use home-brewing devices but would like to learn. Take advantage of this and hold an informal, drop-in one-hour evening or Saturday session each month for customers who want to know more about proper home-brewing principles. For example, you can explain how to use a moka pot and grind coffee correctly for this type of brewer. You can also teach attendees how to grind coffee for use in a French press, and teach small but important details they must know to make great coffee using these brew systems.

You can demonstrate how to use their home espresso machines correctly, how to extract a shot of espresso and how to steam and foam milk. Your own experience has given you an endless amount of material you can present to your customers. By offering these informal demonstrations, you'll see an increase in small ware and bean sales as well.

In-store trainings are a win-win situation. If you offer them on a regular basis, your customers will know you have a passion for coffee and that you want to share it with them. Your demonstrations also benefit your marketing program because your students will tell their friends about what they learned and you may attract new customers. The big chains often don't have the time to invest in this type of activity, so take advantage of your ability to do so. Become known as your community's "Passionate Coffee Experts!"

Signage

No matter how many great coffee and drink specials you advertise, without proper signage customers will be unaware of your offers. And your promotions will likely be unsuccessful. Use plastic table tents and signs on your counter to advertise your specials. If a promotion is big enough, hang banners outside your building, in your windows or behind your bar. If you have a Web site, use it to your advantage and announce classes, specials or new items to Internet surfers.

For big promotions, you may want to invest in short TV or radio spots. Consider advertising in your local papers. The purpose of any promotion is, of course, to get the word out that your operation is ever changing and on the cutting edge of specialty coffee.

Chapter 16

Marketing Against the Chains

Chains Have Real Advantages

Executives of large chains realize the specialty coffee bar is not a fad, and they are going after the profits with all the resources at their disposal — the investment capital, the management experience and the buying power. Some small operators scoff at big businesses that move slowly and have a hard time innovating, but you have to take them seriously. They are coming after your customers.

Big companies can buy out small chains and service these stores at a lower cost than the old owners could. Big businesses have the resources to purchase large volumes at the lowest possible cost and they own warehouses to store what is not immediately needed. With advanced computer systems, they supply their outlets "just in time," to minimize overstock. And because their suppliers want the big volume business, their buyers can negotiate serious discounts. The result is that big buyers always pay less than you will, for everything. That means you will make a little less on every transaction in your store.

As a small independent you have no choice but to market against large chains with some powerful advantages.

What big chain executives can't do is interact with customers each day, to gain a feeling for the pulse of the community. They may live thousands of miles away and know individual stores only through accounting documents. There is no way they can offer the personal touch that you can as a local owner. This is your largest competitive edge, so take advantage of it.

Consolidation

Because of the advantages of being large, many businesses, including the specialty coffee industry, have undergone a period of consolidation over the past decade or two. I don't believe this trend is going to end in the foreseeable future. Medium-sized chains bought small chains and large chains bought medium chains. Sometimes consumers don't realize the boutique coffee bar they visit is now part of a big chain.

You are playing against the giants now and you're heading for trouble if you merely coast along in your comfort zone. As a small independent you have no choice but to market against large chains with some powerful advantages. You won't have the buying power and skilled professional marketing staff and advertising budgets that they have, so you have to make your business special and be sure customers notice. But don't get over-confident and leap into the fray. Try out ideas on a small scale first. Track and test results before investing more time and money. You may discover that what works in Walla Walla won't work in Witchita.

Store Design

Without a doubt, you can often design a more attractive and comfortable store than your chain competition. Begin by assessing what your customers want. There is an expensive urban neighborhood in Portland, Oregon, filled with upscale loft homes and coffee-savvy residents. Independent coffee retailers in the area have studied these residents and found they want warmth and comfort in a coffeehouse. A large chain also has a store in the area, but its generic design ignores the character of its local customers. Design your store to fit the lifestyle of your customers, and you'll already be one step ahead of the chains.

Quality is Your Competitive Advantage

Quality products and service are where the small operator can really compete. First, you can take more care in hiring your employees than the chains. Then, you can put your baristas and other staff through a careful training program instead of the quick cookie-cutter course that many chains use. That will assure they know how to prepare the best drinks.

When I spoke to a woman who managed for one of the largest coffee chains in America, she told me she was taught numerous procedures in the company's training program that she discovered were incorrect when she worked with a Bellissimo consultant years later. She was perplexed: "How is it possible I worked for this company for more than six years and thought I knew coffee and yet I found out later I didn't understand the product at all?"

Set yourself apart from the chains by motivating each of your employees to feel the same passion for coffee that you do.

Train, train, train your employees! Demand they become coffee experts. Set yourself apart from the chains by motivating each of your employees to feel the same passion for coffee that you do. Not only will knowledge and a good attitude inspire a barista to create unparalleled coffee beverages, but it will also result in his or her ability to pass this knowledge on to your customers. The chains don't stand a chance in this area.

Our free enterprise system gives you immense opportunities. But to reap the benefits of that freedom requires the highest level of personal responsibility. If you know exactly how much your top quality products cost, and can deliver them perfectly prepared at a fair price, you can not only compete and survive, but make excellent profits. It's not easy, but smart competitors do it every day.

Everyone Loves Their Special Place

The biggest advantage you have over the chains is your ability to create an operation that has its finger on the pulse of the community you are serving.

Most people don't care which auto shop they visit for a brake job. In many retail arenas choice is based on price. A local retailer or a large chain can provide the simple product or service needed. In many sectors and industries a small start-up is at a gigantic disadvantage competing against a major chain that produces million-dollar commercials to convince the public that their product is superior.

Would you open a clothing store in a large mall, name it PAG and attempt to compete with the GAP? It would be difficult, if not impossible, to compete with this established chain. You wouldn't have the brand identity or the buying, marketing and training power of a large clothing chain. Your chance of success would be small. However, because unique ambiance and superb product quality can predictably draw customers away from the chains, coffee is one industry where you can compete with the chains and win.

Why is coffee retail different? I think it is because coffee people are unique. Our customers love to have a special place where they can hang out with friends. If you listen, you might overhear this bit of conversation in a little neighborhood coffee bar: "Do you still go to the chain coffeehouse on the corner? I used to think their coffee was good until I tasted the coffee here." "Right, this coffee is so much better. It doesn't have that bitter taste. And it's nice to see people smile and care about me. I certainly never got this kind of service at that other place. Why would I go back there?"

Coffee has become deeply ingrained in our society. Of course, as a beverage it tastes wonderful, but the popularity of specialty coffee runs much deeper than that. It's easy for most Americans to buy great beans, purchase wonderful brewing devices and prepare coffee each morning at home in a matter of minutes. Why then do coffee drinkers go to a coffeehouse and pay two to three dollars for something they can prepare at home for a fraction of the cost?

The answer isn't found in chemistry or physics books that explain proper brewing principles; it's found in the textbooks of sociology and psychology. Earlier, I mentioned a book by sociologist Ray Oldenburg, The Great Good Place: Cafés, Bookstores, Bars, Coffeeshops, Hair Salons and Other Hangouts at the Heart of Community. He describes the "third place," which he defines as a place people congregate to find a sense of community outside of the home and workplace. By nature, humans need places where they can meet friends or take solace in the familiarity of other people and their surroundings.

In America, bars serving alcohol have historically been the primary third place. From the saloons we see in early television westerns to modern-day hip watering holes, bars were once the only option for people to meet and socialize. The problem with bars for many people is alcohol. Not everyone wants to achieve an altered state of mind, and the stigma surrounding bars has grown with the enactment of stricter drunk-driving laws and increased concern about the potential health risks of alcohol. The coffee bar is the perfect alternative. And you can still serve beer and wine without giving your coffeehouse the feel of a tavern.

The answer isn't found in chemistry or physics books that explain proper brewing principles; it's found in the textbooks of sociology and psychology.

In the early years of this industry, Roger Sandon, founder and publisher of Café Olé Magazine, said to me, "It's not about the coffee...it's about the break." Another Seattle friend and coffee bar owner, Italian-born Mauro Cipolla, has echoed the same sentiment. Cipolla asserts that while the coffee in Italy is excellent, the reason there are more than 200,000 coffee bars in that country is because they provide a place to meet friends and neighbors. These small bars on nearly every corner are where you learn that your close friend's wife is pregnant, someone's uncle is ill or hear the score of last night's soccer match.

North America is finally catching on to Europe's well-established third place culture. In the past ten years, coffee establishments have played a major role in satisfying the inner need of Americans for a third sanctuary. A good friend of mine who moved to a bedroom community in Seattle was more thrilled with the local coffee bar on the corner than with her beautiful apartment with a view of Lake Washington.

> **Your coffee establishment has a much better chance than a chain operation of becoming your neighborhood's – or even your city's – third place.**

Each time I called her, she talked more about the coffee hangout than any other part of her life. A group of people met there each morning before work, and she soon spent hours socializing with the group almost every Saturday and Sunday morning. This is a woman who is involved in the coffee industry and can brew a great cup at home. But within the confines of her kitchen, she can't brew the friendship or fulfill the need we all have as humans to share and interact with others.

Your coffee establishment has a much better chance than a chain operation of becoming your neighborhood's — or even your city's — third place. You know your community and the people who live there. You understand what they want and you can fulfill their needs better than an operation that was conceived in some Manhattan high rise.

Lay the Publicity Groundwork

The giants leave nothing to chance. As soon as they lease a space, they make a big announcement to the press and local media, and let it be known they are hiring now. They use ads, flyers and posters on campuses and in the still-unfinished windows of the future coffee bar. With great fanfare, they announce a preview night and invite local bigwigs and media people for a gala formal or casual party and free samples. Of course they invite the TV news crews. Soon everyone in town knows the place is opening, and the preview night gives staff a chance to practice what they know.

You may feel that a festive opening event is beyond your budget. But your opening is news, so get the word out. If you aren't a wordsmith, you may discover a writer or publicist on your staff. You'd be wise to pay a person extra for well-developed skills and the ability to see the whole project to completion. See Chapter 18 for more on publicity.

Use a snappy, very clear and simple one-page press release with a clever hook in the first line. Offer to be interviewed. Provide complete contact information so reporters can call you for details. Call editors to see if they accept press releases, and to find out what they want and when they want it. Ask if they want artwork. And to whom should you address your envelope? Then send your release to all appropriate radio and TV stations and the daily and weekly newspapers that cover your area. Don't ignore the ethnic media if you're in a community rich in immigrant cultures. Many harried reporters, especially at smaller papers, quote press releases almost verbatim to generate copy on deadline.

After you've opened, use the news to get attention and announce changes. Create events such as celebrations, guest presentations, film showings or classes. They give you something to talk about, a reason for the media to notice you again. Media coverage may not put out all the details you'd like people to know, but research shows it has higher credibility than advertising. And it costs you far less.

> The specialty coffee business represents billions in profits annually, but small players can still claim a share.

The time to start planning your marketing against the giants is well before you open. Be smart and be organized, with a detailed calendar of things to do. And be fearless, so that you're not just another dull business owner looking for attention without a story to tell.

The specialty coffee business represents billions in profits annually, but small players can still claim a share. Competition just raises the stakes and makes everyone sharper. Compete in this challenging arena knowing that if you think smart and use the skills you've honed to perfection, you have a great chance of standing up to Goliath.

CHAPTER 17

GUERRILLA MARKETING INSIDE YOUR CAFÉ

I'm not sure how the term "Guerrilla Marketing" originated. I do know it was made famous by Jay Conrad Levinson, who produced a fine series of guerrilla marketing books including *Guerrilla Marketing Excellence* and *Guerrilla Marketing: Secrets for Making Big Profits from Your Small Business*. Levinson also has an on-line marketing magazine, at http://www.guerrillamarketinga ssociation.com. He says it takes nine exposures to your marketing, during which you transform apathy into a trusting relationship, before a new prospect can be expected to actually buy anything from you.

Guerrilla means little warrior and refers to insurgents who challenge a powerful government. In an attempt to topple the existing regime, they fight in the streets against well-armed militia, using rocks or bottles filled with gasoline. History proves guerrilla fighters can win against amazing odds, including against that coffee gorilla on the corner.

The guerrilla wins by being faster and smarter and thoroughly knowing the local terrain.

When you fight the mega coffee chains, you can't beat them at their own game. You have to redefine the rules. The guerrilla wins by being faster and smarter and thoroughly knowing the local terrain. Marketing is as much art as science, and it has to be the most creative part of your business and constantly changing. Everything you do must set your coffee bar apart as a unique place with the best possible products. Use your imagination. Tap into your staff for ideas, get online and scour those marketing materials, books and Web sites for ideas you can use.

You can't buy the costly "weapons" the big guys use to win. Could you afford to place a full-page ad in the local newspaper for your newest line of tea? No. It's not cost effective for you to spend thousands of dollars to buy that ad space. And you can't afford a Madison Avenue firm to create a radio and television advertising campaign. Does this mean you are doomed? No! You can win the hearts and minds of the people in your area, because they are your customers and you know them better than the mega chains that run their operations out of a corporate office a thousand miles away.

Encourage People to "Buy Local"
If given the option, most of us will patronize homegrown businesses. People like to buy products and services produced where they live. A successful store in my state is called "Made in Oregon." From handmade jewelry to Oregon wine, people love to buy gifts there for out-of-state friends and relatives. Like most people, Oregonians are proud of their state and feel a kinship with the unique products made there.

Your customers will take the same sort of pride in knowing that even though the coffee beans you serve were grown on the other side of the world, the profits from selling them will stay in their community. Reread Chapter 13 on Branding and Identity for more ideas on how to create an ambiance, menu and overall marketing plan based on the fact that you are a local entrepreneur and not a cog in the mega chain.

Ask for Word of Mouth
Word of mouth has long been known as the very best form of publicity for any business. The fact that it's free is a major factor in its favor also. If people hear about your business from someone they trust, the message is believable. A happy customer will be glad to tell friends about you, your coffee and your operation.

Train your employees to ask regular customers to be sure to let others know how much they like your drinks and the atmosphere. Add a reminder to all your printed materials, and even your signage. "Tell your friends how much you like us."

Hold on to Current Customers
It's a given that it costs much more to recruit someone new than to retain an old customer. But customers move, change jobs and can drift away if you don't let them know how much they mean to you. You can keep in touch when you have obtained their names and contact information, thanks to your database.

Send your regular customers thank-you notes. That will show your appreciation and make you stand out from nearly all other businesses. Let them know about offers and your Web site. Invite them to special events. Encourage them to talk about you and to bring friends in. And always greet them by name when you can. Show them you appreciate their loyalty.

> **If people hear about your business from someone they trust, the message is believable.**

Market to Your Neighbors
A coffee bar is a neighborhood gathering place and a valuable resource for the people nearby. Even if you're not ready for cross marketing, when you open, visit other businesses on the block and provide them with a written invitation to stop in. If you have a grand opening, be sure they are invited. Provide some special offer

coupons for employees. Let them know the hours you'll be open and encourage them to stop by for a drink or good food before, after or during working hours. You want them to get used to coming in often, since you are so conveniently located close to them.

Once you have made allies of neighboring businesses, you can more easily approach managers with ideas for strategic alliances, shared marketing, planning and creating other win-win projects.

Guerrilla marketing ideas are as unlimited as an active imagination.

Small Ideas With Big Results

Guerrilla marketing ideas are as unlimited as an active imagination. Some we've seen work well include offering gift cards or discounted prepay cards good for a dozen lattes or other drinks. Not every good idea out there will work for you, but you only need a few that click to boost your profits. The important thing is to keep at it. You have to promote yourself every day, every week, all month and all year.

Deliver free coffee and pastries to the DJs at popular morning radio shows and live remote broadcasts. Do a coffee tasting at a health club or gym. Print business cards for your whole staff and encourage them to hand them out. Give customers a free drink on their birthday. Supply the coffee for a neighborhood event. Post copies of interesting coffee-related magazine articles.

Have a guest book where people can sign in, provide personal information and add comments. If you run a contest, post the names of winners and what they won. Adopt a cause your customers support. Join the Chamber of Commerce and network with other business owners. Put up colorful seasonal banners. Thousands of guerrilla marketers have increased their bottom line using these and other creative, low-cost ways to get noticed, because they work.

Plan to include bigger ideas in your marketing strategy also. You can execute most of these on a limited marketing budget and, if done with passion and planning, most will pay off big in terms of profits.

Create a Database

How many times have you seen a fish bowl filled with business cards on the counter of a business? Do you wonder why these establishments want your card?

Business cards tell you who your customers are, so you can use the information to create a database and send customers promotions, information on special events and specials. With their e-mail addresses, you can send out an Internet newsletter every month, a mailing filled with practical and interesting information about coffee. Make it attractive and interesting, with material worth their time, then use this clout to lure them back to your coffee bar by announcing new offers and events.

Why not use technology to make the task of harvesting information even easier? Bellissimo had a client in Pensacola with experience in the computer industry. He purchased a hand-held scanner, then asked customers if they wanted to receive his Internet newsletter and special mailings. He would zip his scanner over their business cards, then each evening one of his employees downloaded the information into the main database. Within a few months our client had collected over 2000 names. He sent his well-crafted mailings to all of them. Within six months his operation was thriving, thanks in part to his mailings, even though his location was mediocre at best.

Whether you collect names from cards in a fish bowl, use a scanner or sign-up sheets for prizes, you can encourage more customers to give you their personal information. As a reward, you might give away a free pound of coffee, logo T-shirt or small French press. For the Pensacola retailer, the total cost of collecting hundreds of leads a week was amazingly low.

Don't Forget the Kids

When you think marketing, think about children too. Parents may be hard pressed to find a family-friendly third place where they can relax and meet friends. Create a menu of kids' drinks so your customers' children look forward to coming. Many parents who are craving a latte might otherwise have to settle for cola or a really bad coffee at a child-friendly hamburger joint, if they have their children with them.

If you have the space, and it fits your image, create a children's play area in your café. The man who scanned business cards designed a small area in the rear of his store that was filled with games and children's books. A community café in Alaska showed old movies and offered free popcorn every Saturday at three, and drew a crowd of parents and kids at an hour when few had visited before.

Give youngsters a good reason to talk their parents into bringing them to your store.

If your goal is to attract kids and their families, consider an ad in the local school paper or a flyer announcing an event, to be posted at school or the YMCA, or other place where lots of kids congregate. Give youngsters a good reason to talk their parents into bringing them to your store.

For the Readers

Keep a few daily newspapers and recent magazines on hand for those who come in without anything to read or to work on. Subscribe and make available a labeled CAFÉ COPY of the *Wall Street Journal* or *New York Times* if your customers are likely to read those great papers. An Italian-themed coffee bar in my Portland neighborhood offers at least a dozen colorful, large-format books on Italy for customers to peruse.

Make sure your own materials are always at hand. Set out your catalog, your newsletter, business cards, brochures you develop to answer common coffee questions, and anything else with your message. Offer a special product promotion, or talk up an event in the store. Develop a series of brochures answering frequently asked questions about coffee. Print up a weekly trivia sheet about coffee.

Free Samples

If you want to try giving something away, sometimes coupons are not your best bet. Studies show that the best return on investment comes when you give small free samples of your excellent products. The test is in the taste. You won't have to convince anyone your products are great if you give them a no-risk opportunity to try them. If they like what they taste, they will be back with their friends.

Your Grand Opening
A grand opening is an event that can start you off with a bang. It's your chance to feel proud of what you've achieved in opening this business and your opportunity to invite everyone you know to come admire and enjoy your new coffee bar. Send invitations to business leaders, community celebrities and officials and, of course the media. If you can get a celebrity there, the media is sure to follow. A ribbon cutting could bring out the mayor or local state representative. Offer demonstrations in making the perfect cappuccino. Serve a free beverage and food, and offer a chance to win prizes, which you may get donated if you offer publicity to the donors.

When should you have it? Thursday or Friday night is the best time to catch people on their way home from work, so schedule it for four to nine. A large gala event works best on a weekend. You may need an event planner to help out. Or, start out with developing a series of spreadsheets to keep you organized – guest list, to-do list with steps to take, jobs in sequence, etc. The net expense of an opening event is often only the cost of product and labor. This is an inexpensive way to get people through your door for the first time.

Pick a date with few conflicts with other events, then set a budget. Create your guest list and invitations, do a press release and place ads on radio and in local papers to get the word out. Distribute flyers, put up posters, hand out free-drink tickets good for the day of your opening.

Host Other In-Store Events
You can host numerous events in your space to bring in more customers. But before you make big plans, talk to your current customers and get their feedback. What would they like? Consider live entertainment, in-store classes or poetry readings. Some cafés invite writers to speak about their work and to sell and sign their books. Nearly any community has creative people who are happy to offer a presentation in exchange for exposure.

Coffee Cards, Pre-paid Cards

When I opened my first coffee bar 12 years ago I tried punch cards, also called Preferred Customer Cards. The card I offered gave customers a free drink after they purchased 11 drinks. Having the cards reminds people of you, encourages repeat visits and rewards your regulars. The program was very successful and helped me to build a loyal return customer base.

The latest thing in cards is the pre-sold swipe card. These cards are similar to a credit card and can include your logo, address, telephone number and Web site URL. You can pre-sell these cards in denominations of $5, $10 or $20. These keep customers coming back because they may offer a small discount and people have made a commitment by paying in advance.

Many different types of stores offer these cards because they make great gifts. One reason general retailers love swipe cards is because customers often lose or forget them and never exchange them for merchandise. This should not be your reason for offering swipe cards, but if I were opening a café tomorrow, I would definitely make them available to my customers.

Sales, Loss Leaders and Samples

We've established that people forget about you if you don't remind them frequently. And you need a reason to ask them to notice you again. Earlier, I discussed the importance of always having something on sale. Special offers increase sales. Advertise Mocha Monday or Teapot Tuesday. I hardly ever miss eating at my favorite Mexican restaurant on Taco Tuesday (two tacos, two bucks). It works!

A loss leader is a great offer at a very low price. You lose money on that one item in order to get people in the door, where they will buy other things and get to know your business. Grocery stores use them frequently. For example, you may offer your muffins at half price to customers who purchase a latte. You could also offer a free drink to a regular customer who brings in a friend. This could be especially profitable if the friend becomes a regular.

Free samples can sell a lot of a certain item in a short time or allow your regulars to try something different. Sampling is also a simple and inexpensive form of market research and a good way to find out if a product you are considering is right for your store.

Use Signs and Banners

When you have something to announce, use a large sign or banner visible from the street, and use others inside the café. Keep to the tried and true working principles of good advertising. Remember that no one driving by can take in more than seven words at a glance so use the concepts that make a successful billboard work – keep it very simple, and keep it eye catching with bright colors and a simple graphic image. Inside and outside your café, have all signage conform to your business image with a unified typography and design theme.

Even Big Companies Use Guerrilla Marketing

Entrepreneurs are not the only ones who practice guerrilla marketing. Recently, I went to my bank and everywhere I looked, I recognized guerrilla marketing at work. First, you must understand that this bank doesn't act or look like a bank. It operates more like an upscale boutique. However, its marketing is some of the best I've ever seen.

Sampling is also a simple and inexpensive form of market research and a good way to find out if a product you are considering is right for your store.

The first time I went into the Portland branch, a greeter met me at the door and asked me if I would like a tour of the facility. I was impressed by the offer and said yes. The tour guide was actually there to sell people on the bank's services and special offers. She told me that anyone who opens a business account at the bank receives a book on business each quarter. I have received three of these books since I opened my account and each is worth between $30 and $40. She also told me that those who open personal accounts may choose a gift, either logo hat, T-shirt or pound of coffee.

The bank hired a local roaster to create a special blend for them, and the bank staff is very proud to let people know how fresh their coffee is. Does this give you any ideas for cross marketing?

At this bank every employee "floats" and must know every other employee's job. The bank also features a large area of online computers with beautiful flat screen monitors. The signage over this area says only "SURF." In an adjacent area where hot coffee is made available for customers, the signage simply says "SIP."

My "bank tour guide" asked me what I did for a living. I told her that I was a coffee educator. She said that each Saturday morning the bank invites a specialist to give a talk about his or her area of expertise. After our discussion, I agreed to give a future lecture on coffee, geared toward the coffee consumer. The bank promotes these talks with eye-catching signage. During my visit, I saw signs for an upcoming knitting demonstration, among other events.

Your reaction might be, "Hello, this is a bank and I can't afford to give away expensive books." And you're right. This is a bank and you can't do everything it does. But what can you learn from this example, pulled from an industry about as far away from a coffee bar as one can get? Even large corporations benefit from inexpensive guerrilla marketing (the computer stations, free classes, free coffee and tours). Not only does this type of marketing work, often it works better than advertising that costs millions of dollars.

CHAPTER 18

GUERRILLA MARKETING
OUTSIDE YOUR CAFÉ

Guerrilla marketing outside your café is to remind people who know you that you are an active member of the community, and to tell people who don't that your coffee bar is a great place. The challenge for a business with a small advertising budget is to promote consistently, spend wisely and be creative enough to take advantage of every opportunity to create news and garner the free publicity that brings name recognition.

Use targeted marketing to narrow your aim and raise your effectiveness. You know what your customers want. And unlike some businesses, you know where to find them. Your current and potential customers live, work or shop near you, or frequently drive past your coffee bar. You don't have to reach out to the whole world. But you do have to reach out. Guerrilla marketers have come up with dozens of ways you can generate interest in your business, and most of them cost you little more than some time and effort.

Be a Speaker

My talk at the bank on Saturday ties into a good way to promote your business in your town. Position yourself as an expert. Offer to give talks at libraries, local industry associations and meetings of the Rotary and Kiwanis clubs in your area, and to any other group with members who might become customers. At these events, give out discount coupons for a drink in your coffee bar. Collect business cards as part of a drawing for a pound of superb beans then add these people to your mailing list. Some of them may later offer you unexpected opportunities, such as supplying the coffee for a breakfast meeting at the college or at a conference.

To be a good citizen of your community, you almost have to get involved in causes and events.

Make calls to find out who is in charge of programs and let that person know what you can do and when you are available. The volunteer will most likely be grateful to you for making it easy to find a speaker. If you'd like to quickly improve your speaking skills, join your local chapter of Toast Masters. The more experience you have, the larger and more sophisticated audience you can command.

Sponsor Community Events

To be a good citizen of your community, you almost have to get involved in causes and events. Sponsorship alone does not bring new customers, but it makes your current customers feel good about your role in the life of their community. Look for ways you can put your logo and your business image in front of the people you choose. It's tough to decide between a large number of causes. Choose one you personally believe in, but make sure it's one that targets the right people, be it a black-tie silent art auction or the church spaghetti feed.

Get involved with worthy projects in your own town to generate face time with your target audience. Donate unused, outdated coffee to a shelter house. Be the coffee provider at a fundraiser for the symphony, Habitat for Humanity, the Race for the Cure or local kids' team. Give a gift to an auction to support a halfway house or summer swim program. Invite a radio station to do a special event broadcast from your café. Serve pastries to athletes at the Special Olympics. Offer a partial scholarship, to be announced at a big event. Sponsor a race and get your name on the T-shirts. Hold a contest and donate proceeds to a local group.

If you get involved in a community event, be sure you retain some control over what is said about you, how your logo and image are used, and what other groups your name is associated with. Ask to see advance proofs of printed material and to review tapes for TV and radio. You want to avoid unpleasant surprises. Keep records of all costs and donations, including time and materials contributed. You may be surprised how it adds up in a year. You want your accountant and the IRS to know about these donations, too.

The Power of the Press

You want great stories about you to appear in print or online. So, create your own newsletter. The real power of the press is in the hands of the one who owns one. In your own publication, the message is exactly what you want to say. Here's where your database can really reap rewards. You are sending your information to a targeted audience, already interested in what you are doing and what you have to say.

Include announcements about events at your coffee bar, sales and special price offers, educational stories about coffee, recipes for coffee-related foods, history, cultural material about coffee-producing regions, material on specialty coffees, utensils used in making coffee, organic production, worker co-ops, or methods of coffee processing. Include short bios of your employees and vignettes about funny things that have happened in the café. Invite your regular customers to a showing of a film on coffee, like Bellissimo's "The Passionate Harvest." Announce your in-store classes, seminars and entertainment.

A great newsletter is rich in graphics, eye-catching images and photographs, diagrams and art. Make it a quick read, just a friendly reminder of the fascinating world of coffee and of you as a personal and top quality connection to that world. Continue a story in a jump to a later section to draw people deeper. Keep the print large, the sentences and paragraphs short, the words lively but simple. Active verbs jump and sparkle, while the use of passive verbs can be dull. If you hate to write, here's where you can use the services of a journalism student or a PR professional.

Your Local Press

Never underestimate the power of your pen. Send your local newspaper your press release about any event you want to promote. Better yet, make an appointment and meet the editor of the business section. I have done this time and time again with successful results. You may also find it valuable to connect with the food editor, who might use a story on your special Italian pastries or let you write one on home brewing of the best coffee or on tea for the connoisseur.

A few years ago the local paper contacted Bellissimo about doing a full-page story on our company. Given that 99 percent of our business comes from outside of our small metro area, I wasn't sure I wanted to invest the three or four hours the reporter wanted for an interview. I finally consented because I felt there was a good chance the story would get picked up by a national wire service. I was right. Within the next month, the story ran in over 50 newspapers, including an almost full-page spread in the San Francisco Chronicle.

Editors of local print media and of radio and television news often feature stories about coffee, so do what you can to get them to notice your special project or event. A public relations professional can help you create your strategy and make sure the media pick up the story. As suggested earlier, one coffee company supplies the brew in exchange for some free plugs whenever a radio station does a special event broadcast, be it from the County Fair, the big game or the annual parking lot sale by the car dealership.

Press Releases

If you can think like a reporter, you can turn a simple press release about something you are doing into a story in your local paper. What is the unique angle here? Where is the real news? If you are inviting local dignitaries to a party honoring an employee who spent three months working with coffee growers at an organic farm in Nicaragua, include an anecdote about something remarkable that happened during her stay there. Emphasize the uniqueness of what she did, and the relationship of your business to better living conditions for workers.

A press release that follows a simple formula is likely to be read by an editor and generate interest. Give it a title: "Coffeehouse sponsors better living for struggling farmers." Provide all needed contact information of the person or people to call for more details. Get the pertinent facts into the first sentence or two, preferably with a lively quote. Here's an example.

Sunday, October sixth, Sophia's Coffeehouse will host a gala welcome-home dinner for Janna Samson, honoring their popular long-time barista for her summer of work with coffee farmers in Nicaragua. Samson says, "This will be fun. I'll show a cool film we made and talk about my enriching experiences in an amazing culture."

Call and ask who would be the right person to send it to. Talk to that person. Ask what they want to see and how you can help them. One page double-spaced is plenty, in nearly all cases. Edit until it's tight and concise. Active verbs jump, jangle and shout for action, while the use of passive language is unlikely to be fun. If you have ideas for photographs, mention that.

Send your press release three to four weeks in advance, then call and ask it they received it, not if they intend to run it. Invite them down to your coffee bar. Some papers will use your press release in the form they receive it. Others rewrite and call to fill in details. If the story looks especially intriguing, they may send out a reporter to do a larger article. Any book on advertising and public relations will give you plenty of good ideas, with a variety of examples of what a press release should contain.

When a story comes out, write a thank-you note to the people who made it happen. Create a list of print, radio and TV people who have treated you well and contact them personally next time. Use every newsworthy event to put out the word to them, and to make new media contacts. Save any articles, tapes and video that feature you to build your publicity portfolio. Media people then see you as an expert who's already successful.

Advertise Wisely
The advantage of buying advertising is that you can get across exactly the message you choose. Because advertising is so effective, those who sell it know they can ask top dollar. Your goal should be to match your demographics with your advertising vehicle. Targeted marketing is the only cost effective way to reach your customers, so be sure when you choose a publication or medium it's one they are likely to see or listen to. Properly located billboards can be highly effective, while TV is generally not suitable for a coffee bar and radio is often too expensive.

But don't look at cost alone. One Vermont coffeehouse owner ran his ad in the weekly free Advertiser for many weeks but saw no increase in sales. He felt loyal to them because they produced a display ad at no charge and it cost very little. His customers came from an upscale neighborhood, filled with trendy boutiques. These were not the people who read the Advertiser. When he rethought his strategy, he hired a pro who focused on the people he wanted to reach and saw sales increase.

When do you advertise? A good time is when your chief competition does. Don't let them get ahead of you in this game. Talk about the features and benefits of a special coffee maker, how it will intrigue their friends, accessorize their home. Tie your ad to a season. Tie it to the ethnic holidays of your customers. Make it something to which your particular population can relate.

You will get calls and visits from people selling ads in all sorts of vehicles from radio and TV to regional magazines. Ask to see their demographic information before you place your ad. Are they able to reach your customers? You don't need an expensive publication or TV ad until your customer demographics justify it. If you've done your homework, you know who your customers are and you know right away if a vehicle is right for you.

A Great Example

Bellissimo once had a client who was the owner of a small Pennsylvania coffee company specializing in earth-friendly coffee. This particular client was having trouble getting the press to cover his business, even though he had a beautiful story to tell. At the time we worked with this client, his company was unique because few coffeehouses were selling issue-oriented coffee and supporting organizations like Coffee Kids (www.coffeekids.org). Coffee Kids is an International organization that works to better the lives of children and families in coffee-growing communities.

Finally, after a trip to an Indonesian growing region, the owner wrote a press release about his company and sent it to the local paper along with some color photographs he had taken of people harvesting, sorting and roasting coffee using simple local methods. The regional newspaper sent out a reporter to do a larger story. Employees and customers said the reason they either worked for or patronized the business was the commitment and passion behind the product. After the story appeared, the coffeehouse experienced a significant increase in business.

> Your goal should be to match your demographics with your advertising vehicle.

The next weekend a local television station picked up the story from the newspaper and did a feature on the coffeehouse. The media feeds off each other, TV reporters scanning newspapers for human-interest stories. Many features on the late Friday broadcast will be run on Saturday or Sunday as well. Media people watch each other for good ideas, as do leaders in most businesses. Even a small story in a college paper or alternative weekly may generate interest and get picked up by the larger media.

Door Hangers, Menus, Coupons, Give-aways and More

I owned a small coffeehouse in suburban Portland, set amid dozens of condos and upscale apartment complexes. As part of my guerilla marketing effort, I contacted the managers of each property and offered them a month of free coffee if they would allow me to leave menus or door hangers at their units. Half the time I was turned down, but when I was given permission to leave them, the door hangers resulted in an increase in business that more than paid for the small cost of printing and distributing them.

Bellissimo's first office was in an upscale office park near a shopping center. Each day I walked to a nearby cart operation to buy my morning coffee. The business was struggling, and I felt so sorry for the young couple who owned it that each time I stopped in I gave them a great idea on how to increase their business. The business had the potential to do ten times its then current volume. The first thing I did was to convince them to change to a higher quality coffee. Next, I taught them proper drink preparation techniques. Finally, I worked on their marketing plan.

Thousands of people worked in the buildings surrounding this operation. If the couple could capture a small percentage of these people, their operation would become highly profitable. I suggested they run a monthly special and distribute printed menus. The first week of each month, the husband went to every building and asked each business to post a new menu in their break room. He also gave each receptionist a dozen 50-cent off coupons to pass out to employees. Soon the business went from selling less than 50 cups a day, to selling more than 300.

Some cafés distribute monthly flyers in a similar way. Start with a grabber headline, provide reasons why you are THE quality coffee operation in town, then make a great offer. Distribute these all around your area, even hiring a friendly young person to hand them out on the street. If the customer must turn in the flyer to get the offer, you can count returns to measure your success.

Giving coupons works best when you do it for very specific reasons, like thanking people who helped you. In general, offering a discount attracts a few people but it also lowers the apparent value of your product. When I worked with a café in Virginia, I stopped all their discount programs and emphasized quality and location. People are pleased to pay a premium for the pleasure of a gourmet or boutique experience. In many cases, you can raise prices and still bring in more business. But that takes imagination.

Cross marketing with coupons, on the other hand, is a workable strategy. One Rhode Island coffee bar owner provided coupons to a local video store. The video store said that if you bought a gift certificate for five rentals, you got a coupon for a complementary espresso at the coffee bar. To the buyer of a prepaid card good for drinks, the coffee bar offered a coupon good for a discount on a movie rental. This program benefited both businesses.

Catering to Get the Word Out
Caterers often pay little attention to the quality of the coffee they serve, seeing it as an afterthought, far less important than the food. This leaves a void you may be able to fill. Some coffee businesses have a made a success of offering an espresso bar at catered events or conferences. Many patrons are delighted to have such a pleasant alternative to the alcohol bar at a conference, wedding, medical meeting, or gallery opening.

A typical operation will offer espresso drinks, flavored drinks and some iced drinks. Limit syrup flavors to three or four favorites, which means people make up their minds faster too. Technical glitches can kill you, so before setting up be sure you have the electrical power and water you need. Respect for the client's property will ensure they call you again.

If you want to grow your operation, but are not yet ready to open a second or third store, coffee catering is an option to seriously consider, especially in a good sized urban area where no one is yet doing it, or doing it as well as you can. And the added benefit is that your name gets out into the community, and hundreds of new people discover what excellent products you offer.

CHAPTER 19

INTERNET MARKETING

Any independent specialty coffee or tea retailer would be remiss in underestimating the power of the World Wide Web. Opportunities to enhance, expand and tap new markets are wide open. Hundreds of thousands of people daily access the almost infinite amount of information in cyberspace. "Coffee" is one of the most frequently searched words on the Web.

From consumers to industry professionals, it seems anyone and everyone with an interest in coffee increasingly looks to the Internet for resources and information. When you have a Web site, you have a willing audience. People who visit are there by choice, having searched for a coffee topic or followed links of interest from related sites.

A recent search came up with over 24 million sites that referred to coffee in some way, and nearly two million for "specialty coffee." Most of these pages are professionally written and illustrated, beautiful and enticing. Your competitors are working hard to capture attention in this formidable advertising and marketing medium where small and large businesses have an equal chance of being noticed.

Whether you already have a Web presence or are ready to think about it, do your own Internet search and see what the other coffee businesses are doing online. It's a great way to check out the competition. Visit many sites and follow links to related sites. Like a child, go exploring in this dynamic realm where the latest marketing ideas are on display at the click of a mouse. If you need help, nearly every public library in the country now has a person on staff to help you do research with one of their computers.

The New Marketing

Once, designing a Web site seemed like an impossible task that could only be accomplished by the select few who understood coding with html (Hyper Text Markup Language). Bellissimo's first Web site in 1995 was a three-page, black-and-white 'masterpiece' that cost an enormous amount of money to put online. Because of my ignorance, we did not purchase our own domain name (URL), but had the site attached to our Web developer's URL. The site was never released to any search engines, and I'm not sure anyone ever found it.

Less than a decade after we built our first site, the Web had grown up and was very different. Today, you can hire a company to design your site or you can do it yourself with some fairly inexpensive software. I would advise you to seek help. A talented individual, or a smaller company with lower overhead, can save you a lot of money.

If your coffee operation is small, investing in online marketing should be approached with prudence. Unless you plan to sell items online — coffee beans, mugs and T-shirts — use fiscal restraint and take a simple approach.

On the other hand, selling online gets easier all the time. Once, you had to set up a credit card account but now systems such as Authorize.Net make it secure, simple and inexpensive to get paid. Businesses that sell specialty coffees and related items online have a huge potential for increased sales, but to reap this potential requires a new focus, some knowledgeable help and a commitment to taking your business in a new direction.

Secure your own URL (Uniform Resource Locator, the code name of an Internet logical address). That comes first on your online marketing to-do list. Many companies sell URLs, but I recommend www.networksolutions.com. A screen appears, you enter your desired domain name and it will immediately search and let you know if it's available. Often you will have to try many to find one not taken. At times, a lot of creative imagination is required to get close to what you really want. Sometimes a name is officially taken but is actually not in current use. The cost to own and use a URL starts at about $25 per year, with discounts when you pay for multiple years.

If the name of your coffeehouse is available, by all means, buy it!

URLs are available with different extensions — .net, .org, .biz, and so on — but the most common and desirable extension for a business is .com. Choose a URL that defines your business. If the name of your coffeehouse is available, by all means, buy it! When you own it, print your Internet address on all your promotional materials. It is as essential as your telephone number. Use the URL wherever your company name and logo appear.

To host your site, you will need to find an Internet Service Provider (ISP) at a cost ranging anywhere from $6.95 to $25 dollars a month.

You can also locate this service via the Web site that offers to verify your URL choices. An ISP will provide access to the Internet and store your Web site on their large computer called a server. They also offer e-mail, and File Transfer Protocol (FTP) access so you can easily update your site yourself when you need to make changes. You can choose an ISP that is based in your community or one that caters to a national clientele. Local service providers can be found in your yellow pages or on the Internet. My company, Bellissimo, has its sites hosted by a local ISP because we like the personalized service we receive.

> **A good designer will create a Web site that is both eye-catching and easy to navigate.**

The Benefits

A short tally of the advantages of having an Internet presence will emphasize why this is an essential part of your marketing strategy. Online, information presentation is dynamic and interactive. The design and presentation of your message is far more flexible than print media, the cost is lower and it's easy to update and to change content. Your site is open "24/7" allowing you to promote your business at your customer's leisure, advertising your business to anyone, anyplace on earth. And, tracking visitor numbers and which pages they access allows you to use your site for market research.

Building It

Every successful Web site shares similar features. Information is clear and well organized. Navigation is intuitive and simple. The host is reliable. It's updated frequently and offers unique information. And, to enhance your marketing strategy, it's set up so that you can use it to collect data.

A good designer will produce a Web site that is both eye-catching and easy to navigate, the two critical factors. Study some sites you think are well done and see what makes them attractive and functional. Your home page should define your business concept, promote your image and contain the most important information you want your customers to receive. Interior pages should have a menu bar, usually a column of links on the left side, allowing visitors to quickly jump to topics of immediate interest on other pages of the site.

Use your logo and branding prominently at the top of your home page and throughout the site. Show pictures of the inside and outside of your coffee bar or teahouse. Include a mission statement defining your business. Your home page should contain your nitty-gritty information, including hours of operation, phone number, e-mail address to contact you, and location. It's smart to include a map or a link to Mapquest or Yahoo! Maps, so people can easily find your café.

Encourage customers to say great things about your operation on comment cards in the store. You can use the best of these flattering e-mails on a testimonial page to show how popular your business is. Provide an e-mail address so they can get their private comments to you. When customers have a question or concern about your business, they can reach you directly.

You'll need to do updates frequently to ensure that the information on your site is current. Unlike alterations in printed ads and marketing materials, changes to your Web site can be done quickly and at little cost. This can be the job of a Webmaster. Or you or one of your computer savvy employees can take on the task.

A site that people want to return to, and bookmark as a favorite, is one that gives them something of value. Go for substance. Cutting-edge graphics will draw people into your site and invite them to explore it, but great content is your real goal. With excellent information, people will linger and also return. Consider offering them something for visiting — a contest, a special report or a chance to download and print out a coupon for a weekly discount.

Be Fun and Informative

If you offer live entertainment at your coffee bar or teahouse, create a "Calendar of Events" page to show who will be playing and when, and then briefly describe the type of music your customers can expect to hear. If you're going to charge a cover, list the amount. Similarly, if your business houses a gallery or features rotating work by local artists, create a page that lists the schedule of shows as well as images of the work, if possible.

Another great idea is to create a page called "Our Baristi." Include short bios and photos of your employees. This is fun for both your employees and your customers. Devote an entire page to your menu so readers know what you have to offer. You might also want to include informational pages to educate your customers. For example, you could create pages on "History of Coffee" or "Proper Home Coffee Preparation." These let your readers know you care about coffee and value your customers. Links to pages of coffee trade shows, educational sites on coffee and coffee publications will also enrich your site.

Marketing to Your Area

You may wish to use your Web site to market your business to a specific town or metro area. Someone in Detroit has little need to find out about your coffee operation in Tucson, Arizona. That's why, when you develop your site, you will need to include your city in the title, key words and a description in the header area of your home page. These should tell people who you are and your key words should narrow down the specifics of your business. For example, if your coffeehouse is in Tucson you should include the key word "Tucson coffeehouse," so people looking for a coffeehouse in your area can find you.

Build it then Link it

Once your site is up on the Web, you will need to do all you can to make sure people visit it. Use relevant key search words to register your site with big search engines that comb the Web for pertinent sites. You want to see your site come up when people query using any of the popular directories and search engines — Google, MSN, America Online, Yahoo, etc. That's the way people find you.

In addition, work to set up reciprocal links with other Web sites of similar interest. You may want links to the sites of your suppliers, local attractions and more.

Keep your Web site fresh. That doesn't mean changing your template and design. Updating can be as simple as announcing your Christmas special or removing outdated announcements promptly. One month, you could announce the special coffee from Papua New Guinea that just arrived at your store. The next month, talk about and show pictures of your extraordinary ceramic mugs from Italy.

Today, the Internet is a tool with far-reaching possibilities. It's an inexpensive way to market your operation, to find new customers and keep loyal ones. The Internet grows more powerful each day, month and year. It can help your business in immeasurable ways.

From a smart marketing standpoint, you must have a Web site. I highly recommend seeking qualified professional services if you want to develop an Internet presence or analyze and assess the value of your existing Web site. I hired professionals to create and maintain my Web presence. I don't have the time or the skill myself and, chances are, neither do you. Success has to be measurable in terms of profits, and while hiring a pro is not a guarantee, it does improve your chances of realizing a greater return on your investment.

If you don't already have a Web site, create one. You can be sure your smart competition will.

CHAPTER 20

THE TIME IS NOW

Marketing is extremely important to any new or existing coffee operation, far more important than to most other businesses. People expect a "cutting-edge" experience in a coffeehouse. With smart marketing, you can let them know your business can give them just that.

Chapters 1 and 2 emphasized the necessity of promoting your operation in the face of increasingly sophisticated customers and competition. All forms of marketing including public relations and advertising aim to raise your profits. Marketing works. If it didn't, businesses would not put so much effort into it.

In Chapter 3, I talked about the importance of knowing your customer. These are the people who must walk through your door each day in order for you to keep your business open. You must know who they are so you can give them what they want.

Chapter 4 covered the importance of developing a unique menu to keep your customers coming back. Your menu must not only be well designed, balanced, creative and unique, but it must also be good...no, actually, it must be great.

If, as stated in Chapter 5, "everything must be perfect," and when something about your operation isn't, your customers may look elsewhere for that ideal place to get a cup of coffee. Strive for perfection!

In Chapter 6 and 7 I told you that your employees are the face of your business and play a vital role in your success. Hire the right people and they may be the reason your customers return day after day. A friendly smile is as much a part of your marketing program as your logo. You must take care of your staff and teach them proper service principles and how to love coffee. They are the disciples who will spread your gospel to others and allow your business and our industry to grow.

If you sell whole-bean coffee and retail items such as brewers, as discussed in Chapters 8 and 9, then you will need to train your employees in selling techniques, proper brewing principles and the nuances of different origin coffees. If you sell and market environmentally friendly coffee, addressed in Chapter 10, then employees will need to understand the different types of issue-oriented coffee on the market so they can intelligently answer your customers' questions.

Whether you are in the planning stages or already open, try new products. Consider expanding your drink menu and maybe even offering some food items. In Chapter 11, I talked about the ever-changing idea of what a coffee bar or café should or could sell. If you are in the right area and have a unique concept, let your imagination and vision lead you. However, your main focus should always be great coffee. Don't confuse your customers about who you are or what you stand for. The quality of your coffee is what they will remember about you. That said, push the envelope and try some new products. Remember the retail mantra — "Grow or die."

Chapters 12 and 13 look at the way your ambiance and business image will project who you are and define the type of customer you want to attract. If your bar is classy and located in an upscale neighborhood, then you must appeal to the customer who enjoys this kind of atmosphere and sophistication.

Chapter 14 teaches you how cross marketing can work for you. Be a friend to your neighborhood and realize your success will be built with a little help from your friends. Give back to your community and make your business an integral part of the place where you live. Word of mouth is the most effective advertising on earth. This has never changed and never will.

In Chapter 15, we looked at how special promotions and events can bring in customers. Chapters 16,17 and18 discussed ways to compete with large chains by focusing on quality and running effective promotions and specials. Use your limited budget and become a guerrilla-marketing expert. Chains often ignore the small details, and this is an area in which you can excel.

In today's modern age, people use the Internet for almost everything. In Chapter 19, I recommended that you build a Web site and introduce your business to the online community. Once you have spent the money to develop your site, the cost of maintaining your online presence will be very small compared to the exposure it will bring to your business.

So what are you waiting for? Great marketing will drag more dollars to your bottom line. It's time to get started!

Bellissimo has been a firm believer in the success of the independent coffee retailer from the day our company opened for business. Today we believe even more strongly that success is possible for the small- to medium-size retailer because, quite frankly, more sophisticated people are getting into this business.

Don't wait another day to market smarter. The time is now!

About the Author

Bruce Milletto is President of Bellissimo, Inc. and Founder of The American Barista and Coffee School. His early involvement and insights into the American gourmet coffee movement have been written about in numerous national and international industry trade publications, where Mr. Milletto has been hailed as a pioneer of the American espresso industry and dubbed "Mr. Espresso USA."

The media frequently call upon Mr. Milletto for information about the specialty coffee industry. He has been interviewed by, or quoted in, *The New York Times, Kiplinger's, Forbes Magazine, Harvard Management Update, Crain's Business Review, The Seattle Times, Time Magazine, The Oregonian, The Washington Post, Entrepreneur Magazine and The Wall Street Journal*. His expert commentary has been heard on the radio, including *Coffee Talk* on the National Public Radio affiliate KUOW in Seattle. In 2003-2004, Mr. Milletto appeared on an HGTV (Fine Living Network) television series that aired on the cable station and on the United Airlines in-flight service network.

Mr. Milletto holds an undergraduate degree from Northern Arizona University and a master's degree from the University of Oregon. He has worked for various corporations and government agencies in marketing and teaching positions. He has owned three successful retail gourmet coffee operations and has assisted numerous clients in creating new coffee start-ups worldwide. As a consultant, he has worked with individual and corporate clients in Asia, Mexico, Europe, the Middle East and North America.

In 2003, the Specialty Coffee Association of America (SCAA) named Mr. Milletto one of its 20 "Coffee Luminaries," and in 2004, he appeared on *The Gourmet Retailer*'s list of the 25 individuals who helped shape the specialty coffee industry. Mr. Milletto was the recipient of the SCAA's Distinguished Author Award in 1999. He serves on the prestigious editorial board of the Specialty Coffee Journal, covering the marketing segment of the specialty coffee industry, and a coffee-product review panel for NSF International, an independent, not-for-profit, third-party standards development and certification organization specializing in public and environmental health. Mr. Milletto serves on, and is the former Vice Chair of, the SCAA Communication Committee. He writes frequently for such trade publications as *Fresh Cup Magazine*, *Fancy Food Magazine*, *Coffee and Beverage Magazine* (Canada), and *Euro Coffee* (Italy). Mr. Milletto was the keynote speaker at the first Greek Coffee Industry Forum in 2001 and has spoken at various other trade shows in both the United States and Europe.

In addition to writing this book, Mr. Milletto is the co-author of *Bean Business Basics*, a 670-page start-up/operational manual. He is also an award-winning film producer/director of coffee-industry films. In 2001, the Bruce Milletto/Kenneth Davids production, "The Passionate Harvest," won Best of Show at Coffee Fest Las Vegas and Best New Product at the 2001 Specialty Coffee Association of America Conference and Exhibition. The film won a Bronze Award at the 22nd Annual Telly Awards, a Silver Award at the 2001 Summit Awards, the Award of Distinction at the 2001 Videographer Awards and a Platinum Award at Worldfest Houston 2001.

Bellissimo Products and Services

Consulting
Bellissimo is dedicated to the growth and success of the specialty coffee industry. The focus of our consulting division is to assist individuals in all aspects of creating new coffee businesses and to provide counseling beneficial to existing operations. Our worldwide client list includes Fortune 500 companies as well as American and international entrepreneurs.

Our team possesses over 75 years of combined experience in retail business ownership, food-service management and specialty coffee. We fully understand every aspect of creating a coffee business and operating it successfully. This expertise is included in our 670-page coffee start-up/operational manual, *Bean Business Basics*.

Over the past 12 years Bellissimo has assisted major companies in developing specialty coffee programs and have helped over 500 individuals with the creation of their coffee businesses. We have also worked with numerous established operators to solve operational problems. We have personally owned retail coffee bar, coffee cart, coffee drive-thru and coffee kiosk operations.

Bellissimo has references who will validate our credentials as qualified coffee-business consultants. The Specialty Coffee Association of America, *Fresh Cup Magazine*, and *Coffee and Beverage Magazine* (Canada) and numerous respected companies frequently refer individuals to us for assistance with the creation or refinement of their coffee businesses. Client references are available upon request.

Some of our Services Include:
- Concept Development
- Logo Development
- Equipment Selection
- Beverage Preparation
- Location Selection
- Staff Hiring & Training
- Vendor Selection

- Menu Planning
- Business Plan Development
- Café Design
- Advertising & Marketing
- Merchandising
- Operational Systems
- Management Training
- Goal Setting
- Business Expansion
- Plumbing & Electrical
- Specifications
- Health Department Dialog
- Grand-Opening Assistance

The American Barista and Coffee School

The American Barista and Coffee School (ABC's), brought to you by Bellissimo Coffee InfoGroup, is the first school in the country devoted to coffee business education and hands-on barista training. At ABC's, students will learn in both a classroom and lab setting the fundamentals of successful coffee business management and proper beverage and food preparation techniques. Classes include a 5-day intensive seminar for new start-ups, a two-day seminar for existing retailers, a three-day, hands-on workshop for baristas, and specially designed seminars for corporations. In the future, ABC's will offer origin retreats, Barista Slams, maintenance and repair seminars and special classes for food and beverage directors, micro-roasters and consumers. Visit www.coffeeschool.org for class schedules, pricing and information on planning travel.

State-of-the-Art Facilities

ABC's has a state-of-the-art classroom where its students will benefit from the latest technologies including PowerPoint interactive presentations. Our lab features the latest espresso and brewing equipment in addition to a granita machine, triple blender station and panini area. Our lab is stocked with the latest products to help students experiment, learn and grow.

Books

Bean Business Basics
$199.95

Are you considering opening a specialty coffee business? Do you already own an existing operation? Are you realizing the level of success you had hoped for?

Bean Business Basics is a 670-page start-up/operational manual that serves as a definitive guide for those starting a retail coffee business and those who have already opened their doors. Bruce Milletto and Ed Arvidson, professionals who have helped their clients open hundreds of coffee bars across the country and around the world, wrote the book. Buying *Bean Business Basics* is like purchasing tens of thousands of dollars of consulting services.

Some of the book's 40 chapters include:
- Coffee Trends
- Proper Brewing Principles
- Basic Espresso Bar Beverages
- Selecting the Right Coffee & Roaster
- Ordering, Handling & Storing Coffee
- Your Financial Resources
- Finding a Great Location
- Codes, Permits & Red Tape
- Negotiating a Lease
- Design & Construction of Your Coffee Bar
- Planning Your Menu
- Choosing & Buying Equipment
- Operational Systems
- Hiring & Managing Employees
- Marketing Your Business
- Record Keeping
- Budget & Cost Controls
- How to Achieve Profitability

Achieving Success in Specialty Coffee
$69.95

In this invaluable book, the most knowledgeable individuals in specialty coffee share their enthusiasm and expertise with the established or new-to-the-market retailer who is serious about operating his or her specialty coffee business at an elevated level and achieving maximum profitability.

Each of the book's 23 chapters is written by a top author or expert in the coffee industry, and is filled with insightful and solid information to help retailers devise their own personal strategies for success.

Dozens of books are available instructing individuals on how to get started in specialty coffee. But few, if any, are available to assist them in profitability once they are open. *Achieving Success in Specialty Coffee* serves as the definitive source for the specialty coffee retailer in the area of operational expertise.

This informative book includes:
- Marketing & Public Relations
- Staff Training
- Equipment Function & Maintenance
- Product Information
- Financial Considerations
- Management Techniques

Opening A Specialty Coffee Drive-Thru
$129.95

Coffee drive-thrus are the fastest growing niche in the specialty coffee market. Written as a concept-specific supplement to *Bean Business Basics*, this manual is dedicated to the unique and exciting drive-thru segment of the coffee business. It contains invaluable information for business-savvy entrepreneurs on location selection, choosing and constructing a drive-thru, working with subcontractors, creating a business plan, negotiating a lease, day-to-day operations, etc. *Opening a Specialty Coffee Drive-Thru* should help you make your entrepreneurial dream become a reality.

DVDs and Videos

The Passionate Harvest
$79.95

An historic film for the specialty coffee industry! This 60-minute film is the definitive film chronicling coffee from seed to cup. Shot in Guatemala, Brazil, Kona and Ethiopia, "The Passionate Harvest" takes a detailed look at the inner workings of the diverse processes involved in coffee production, emphasizing the enormous amount of effort and care required to produce quality coffee, and high-lighting some of the issues and decision points that affect final cup quality and character. The film won a Bronze Award at the 22nd Annual Telly Awards, a Silver Award at the 2001 Summit Awards, the Award of Distinction at the 2001 Videographer Awards and a Platinum Award at Worldfest Houston 2001.

The New Espresso 101
$89.95

"Espresso 101" is the award-winning professional training tool for you and your employees. This tape will cut the normal 20-hour em-ployee training cycle down to three or four hours. This tool pays for itself with the first employee trained. "Espresso 101 Basic Training" is also available in Spanish. Each package includes a study guide, multiple-choice test with answer key and barista diploma.

"Espresso 101" covers:
- A Brief History of Coffee
- Coffee Bean Roasting & Blending
- Espresso Equipment
- Extracting Espresso
- The Art of Steaming & Foaming Milk
- How to Prepare Espresso Bar Drinks
- Fundamentals of Brewed Coffee Preparation
- Cleaning, Safety & Maintenance

Espresso 501 (Advanced Barista Training)
$69.95

This 75-minute video is an advanced course in coffee and espresso for the specialty coffee industry professional. The perfect companion piece to the award-winning video "Espresso 101," "Espresso 501" provides a detailed understanding of the variables essential to create a superior espresso beverage experience. Respected industry professionals share their knowledge and opinions concerning:
- Important factors related to espresso equipment perfomance
- Attributes of excellent espresso coffees
- Understanding the chemistry and nuances of proper espresso preparation
- Beverage presentation/fancy pours
- Principles of superior customer service

"Espresso 101" shows your employees "how" to prepare perfect espresso drinks — "Espresso 501" tells them "why." A perfect advanced video to show your staff a month after hiring.

Everything BUT Coffee
$79.95

Now coffee business owners and their employees can gain a comprehensive understanding of the non-coffee-related aspects of the business. Learn how to maximize your business sales by offering a variety of complementary foods and beverages.

Free Bonus Section: This tape includes the entire contents of "Customer Service for the Retail Coffee Bar." Keep your customers coming back using the sure-fire methods outlined in this video.

An Evening with the Experts
$99.95

A two-video set that includes four hours of interviews with five of the specialty coffee industry's most highly respected professionals. This video explores in detail factors related to green coffee production, roasting and blending, beverage preparation, and the industry's future. Spend an evening learning from Dr. Ernesto Illy, Mauro Cipolla, Kenneth Davids, Ted R. Lingle, and Don Holly.

Spilling the Beans
$39.95

"Spilling the Beans" is a complete video overview of the specialty coffee business. Spend 40 minutes with the experts learning about investment, profit potential, cost factors, location considerations, and much more.

The Art of Coffee
$19.95

This video teaches the home consumer proper handling and preparation of coffee using a wide variety of techniques. Educate your customers about the exciting world of coffee from seed to cup. Wholesale prices available for retailers. Call for pricing details.

Start-up Packages

Start-up 3-Pack
$249.95

Comprehensive package for starting and running a specialty coffee business. Includes: *Bean Business Basics*, "Espresso 101" and "Spilling the Beans."

Start-up 4-Pack
$299.95

Comprehensive package for starting and running a specialty coffee business. Includes: *Bean Business Basics*, "Espresso 101," "Espresso 501" and "Spilling the Beans."

5-Pack Plus
$349.95

Comprehensive package for starting and running a specialty coffee business. Includes: *Bean Business Basics*, "Espresso 101," "Espresso 501," "Spilling the Beans," "Everything BUT Coffee" and "Customer Service for the Retail Coffee Bar."

Drive-Thru 6-Pack Plus
$479.95

Comprehensive package for starting and running a specialty coffee business. Includes: *Opening a Specialty Coffee Drive-Thru*, *Bean Business Basics*, "Espresso 101," "Espresso 501," "Spilling the Beans," "Everything BUT Coffee" and "Customer Service for the Retail Coffee Bar."

Next-Step 3-Pack
$159.95

A comprehensive package for operating your coffee business at its highest potential. Includes: *Achieving Success in Specialty Coffee*, "Espresso 501," "Everything BUT Coffee" and "Customer Service for the Retail Coffee Bar."

Clip Art

Clip Art: Volumes 1, 2 and 3
Each volume:
$49.95
Any two volumes:
$79.95
All three volumes:
$109.95

Countries of Origin:
$79.95

All three volumes plus Countries of Origin:
$179.95

Sip Art volumes 1, 2 and 3 each contain 100 coffee-related images for the PC or Macintosh. Sip Art Countries of Origin contains 50 images associated with coffee-producing countries. Use these creative images for menus, flyers, advertising, point-of-purchase sales, Web design and labels.

MARKETING NOTES:

MARKETING NOTES:

MARKETING NOTES:

MARKETING NOTES:

Marketing Notes:

MARKETING NOTES:

Marketing Notes:

Marketing Notes:

MARKETING NOTES: